Getting Started in Commercial Real Estate

Ten Step Program to Success!

By

Adam Von Romer, CCIM

and

Patricia O'Connor

Copyright 2013 by The Veritas Real Estate Group, Inc. All rights reserved.

ISBN-13: 978-1491022375   ISBN-10: 149102237X

About the Authors

Adam Von Romer, CCIM

Adam Von Romer, CCIM has been involved in the real estate business since 1983; he obtained a real estate license in Pennsylvania before moving to Florida in the late 1980's. Mr. Von Romer has worked with or trained agents from Century 21, ERA, Homes for Living, Coldwell Banker, ReMax, Better Homes and Gardens, and numerous other residential and commercial real estate companies. To date he has brokered, supervised, or negotiated over $1.6 billion in transactions and specializes in the sale of commercial investment real estate. Mr. Von Romer has authored numerous articles on commercial investment real estate including continuing legal education courses on commercial leasing and commercial finance in Florida. Mr. Von Romer has spoken for the National Association of Industrial and Office Properties, the National Association of Realtors, the Florida Association of Realtors, The Broward Alliance, The Tower Club Real Estate Forum and many other civic and trade organization. He has been a featured guest speaker at the Millionaire Club business roundtable, participated in numerous radio shows and has appeared on television. Mr. Von Romer regularly teaches "Getting Started In Commercial Real Estate" and the "Basics of Commercial Leasing" for the Greater Fort Lauderdale Realtors Association. Mr. Von Romer has been a licensed real estate instructor, licensed mortgage broker and licensed community association manager.

Mr. Von Romer has spent the past 20 years working almost exclusively with institutions and high net worth individuals providing numerous services including workouts, restructuring, audits, short sales, leases, syndications, and loan modifications. Most recently Mr. Von Romer and Adam J. Ouellette, Esq. formed Commercial Capital Advisors, LLC to help commercial investment property owners get the representation they so desperately need. The firm offers full service commercial loan modification/workout services and has strategic alliances with MAI appraisers, tax reduction specialists, cost segregation experts, and environmental, planning and growth management experts.

Patricia O'Connor

Pat O'Connor is a licensed Florida real estate broker, instructor, and owner of The Veritas Real Estate Group, Inc., which she founded in 2004 in Fort Lauderdale. Her company is a licensed real estate school as well as a brokerage firm, and she teaches the Florida Sales Associate Pre-Licensing course on a regular basis. Her real estate transactions include both residential and commercial properties in South Florida, and she was a licensed Florida mortgage broker for seven years.

Prior to relocating to Florida in 2002, Ms. O'Connor was employed as a Vice President of Technology at a number of financial firms in New York City including Lehman Brothers, Merrill Lynch and PaineWebber. She has been teaching adults and developing course material since 1985.

She was an Adjunct Professor at Saint Peter's University in Jersey City, N.J. and an Instructor at Columbia University in New York City. Ms. O'Connor enjoys writing about real estate and financial topics and has extensive experience as a freelance writer. Use the following link to view her current list of published books: http://amazon.com/author/patriciaoconnor.

Table of Contents

Introduction — v

Step 1: Getting Started — 1
    Background — 1
    Training — 1
    Plan — 2
    Control — 2
    Productivity — 3
    Tools — 4

Step 2: Defining Your Market — 7
    Geography — 7
    Product Specialization — 7
    Drive Your Market — 11
    Develop a Property Database — 11
    Listing Sites — 13
    Organizations — 13
    Suggested Reading and Market Reports — 17

Step 3: Making the Cold Call — 19
    Word Emphasis — 19
    Voice Inflection — 20
    Psychological Captivators — 20
    Discussion Topics — 23
    Sample Scripts — 26

Step 4: Keeping the First Appointment — 29
    The Business Development Call — 29
    Data Collection — 34

Step 5: Preparing the Listing Proposal — 37
    Supporting Material — 37
    Annual Operating Statement — 39
    Financial Analysis Overview — 43
    Multipliers — 44
    Cap Rate — 46
    Cash on Cash Return — 49

Financial Calculator	52
Internal Rate of Return	52
Present Value and Net Present Value	54
Financial Management Rate of Return	59
Additional Resources	59

Step 6: Presenting the Listing Proposal — 61
Proposal Package	61
Personality Types	66
Presentation Style	69
Ask for the Listing	71

Step 7: Marketing the Listing — 73
Phone Calls	74
Design Considerations	74
Property Description	75
Sources	76
Frequency	80
Plan	81

Step 8: Presenting the Offer — 83
Letter of Intent	83
Sale and Purchase Contract	84
Negotiations	93

Step 9: Closing the Transaction — 95
Tenants	95
Environmental Issues	95
Documents	98
Procrastination	100
Rules for Engagement	102

Step 10: Starting Over — 105
Referrals	105
Marketing	106
Discipline	108
Hierarchy	108

Appendix I. Confidentiality Agreement — 111

Appendix II. Cooperating Broker's Agreement   **113**

Appendix III. Exclusive Representation Agreement   **115**

Appendix IV. Using the HP 10BII Financial Calculator   **117**

Introduction

The original version of this text was written by Adam Von Romer as an in-house training manual for his new commercial real estate sales associates. When Pat O'Connor read it, she thought it would make a terrific resource for the general public and set about adapting it for publication. It's not the intent of the authors to create the ultimate, completely authoritative training manual for the commercial investment real estate field. Rather, this text gives the brand new commercial real estate professional a sense of what to do first and how to get started in the quickest manner possible.

In the past, real estate transactions were conducted among local participants. The rise of the Internet changed all that, and today's real estate agents negotiate with individuals anywhere in the world. However, although it's true that communication is global, the laws and customs are local.

Therefore, this 10 step program is a road map for getting started in commercial real estate and is NOT intended to offer legal, accounting or licensing advice. The student should rely on his or her broker for guidance as to state and local laws that affect the sale of real property. This program is useful for experienced residential real estate sales people, brand new licensees and investors.

If you are interested in having this material presented as a five-day course for your U.S. or international organization, please contact us at info@adamvonromer.com.

Step 1: Getting Started

I. Background

Real estate is cyclic, whether you're talking about residential or commercial properties. The economy expands and contracts, which affect the buyers' psyche and discretionary income. When the economy is booming, investors have money and are willing to spend it. Entrepreneurs start new businesses and need office space. It's a match made in heaven. However, a bust follows every boom. There can be local factors that trigger a decline in a specific area or national factors can exert a general detrimental effect on the real estate market. If the economy slows, interest rates may increase, businesses may have to downsize or close their doors, and empty storefronts become a common sight in the strip malls. Office buildings start offering incentives to prospective new tenants to replace the bankrupt former occupants. Life can be hard for the real estate agent. However, what goes around comes around, and the market always recovers.

Interest rates are a major controlling factor influencing the demand for residential real estate, but the commercial market is affected more by the availability of credit. During economic slowdowns, the historical tendency is to ease credit requirements in order to stimulate an ailing economy. That didn't happen following the financial meltdown of 2008. The federal government loaned the banks bailout money with the expectation that it would be funneled into lending. However, many lenders held onto much of the money and simultaneously tightened residential mortgage underwriting policies. This double whammy caused the real estate market to collapse even though interest rates were very low. Cash buyers dominated the residential market, and the commercial market stagnated.

The value of a commercial investment is derived primarily from appreciation and subsequent resale price. Positive cash flow contributes to the desirability of a property but buying low and selling high is the ultimate goal of most investors. The value of an investment has little to do with the cost to build it or the price you paid for it. Investment value is the rate of return you make on your invested funds and if it's to be a meaningful measure, this must include the amount of profit that's generated upon resale.

II. Training

Knowledge is power, and the fact that you are reading this text indicates your desire to learn more about the field of commercial real estate investment. This is a great first step, but you will need more than this one book to develop an expertise. We'll get you started on the proper path, and then you need to step up and do the work. Ask your broker for advice when you're stuck, and you might want to consider earning a CCIM (Certified Commercial Investment Member) designation. The CCIM is considered the Ph.D. of real estate designations. The courses aren't cheap, but they are thorough. In addition to the coursework, the CCIM candidate must submit a portfolio of qualifying experience and take a comprehensive exam.

III. Plan

Plan your work and work your plan. You need to prepare an agenda of what you want to accomplish during each business day. If you're not organized in the beginning, it will be harder to change your work habits later. Unless you're very skilled or very lucky, your phone won't be ringing off the hook when you first start. You should have plenty of time on your hands to plan and develop a routine that you can follow.

At first, it's easy to get overwhelmed by the sheer volume of things you need to do. One of your highest priorities should be to develop a database that contains details on the type of properties that interest you; this topic is discussed in depth in a later chapter. For now, be aware that researching properties, taking photographs and identifying owners all take time. However, you can take comfort in the knowledge that there have been thousands, if not millions, of people who have started from scratch just like you.

Try to remember that you're building a business and a career that will last many years. The only way to achieve that goal is to build on a strong foundation.

TIP: Plan to succeed.

IV. Control

The best way to raise the probability of successfully completing a transaction is to have control over the transaction. Control is obtained and evidenced by an exclusive agreement whether that's for a listing or buyer/tenant representation. Your broker is likely to have in-house forms that you're required to use, but the appendices include sample forms to help you understand the material.

Before a listing agent releases financial information for a specific property, the buyer usually has to sign a confidentiality agreement (Appendix I).

If a property is listed in the Multiple Listing Service (MLS), the selling agent must be offered a commission. However, unlike residential real estate, many commercial listings are not in the MLS. Therefore, before you ever show one of these properties, you need to find out if the listing agent is cooperating with the selling agent and offering a commission. You do this by requesting a cooperating broker's agreement from the listing agent (Appendix II). This form discloses the offered commission, and if there's no commission, the listing agent will let you know.

If the listing broker isn't offering a commission, you have to obtain payment from the buyer or else you're working for free. Have your buyers sign an exclusive representation agreement (Appendix III) before you show them any properties. The agreement stipulates that the buyer agrees to work only with you, pay enough so that you earn a specified minimum commission in the event that the seller's commission isn't sufficient, and consents to a one-year protection period. During this period, the buyer is legally bound to pay you a commission for any property that you brought to his notice during the term of the buyer broker agreement. Furthermore, you need this agreement signed even if the listing broker offers a commission. When you show a property to a prospective commercial investor, the listing agent often requests that you register the buyer. Protect yourself and prevent your buyer from being approached directly by the listing agent and "stolen" away from you.

TIP: Always have a signed buyer broker agreement with a one-year protection period.

V. Productivity

One of the challenges that a new agent faces is being able to distinguish between a real transaction and an illusory one that will fritter away your time and not result in a paycheck. Good intentions will get you nothing in this game except frustration. Your time is valuable, and buyers, sellers and other real estate professionals have absolutely no problem wasting your time. After all, it doesn't cost them anything.

If the activity you're engaged in isn't at least 70 percent or more likely to result in a commission check to you within the next 90 days, move on to the next deal. Be brutally honest and realistic with yourself. You must look at all your activity with an eye to whether it's a real transaction or just an amusing and diverting adventure.

VI. Tools

You will need a computer, cell phone, camera, document scanner, financial calculator, spreadsheet software and contact management software. Most of you probably own the first three of these items, but if you've owned them for a few years, they may need replacement or upgrading.

Computer

Desktop, laptop and notebook computers are all suitable for a commercial real estate professional; tablets are not acceptable for the typical sales associate. Most practitioners need to have significant storage capacity, 4 GB or more of internal memory and USB ports to be their most productive. However, the tech-savvy agent may be able to function using only a tablet. Google provides free online storage space and Microsoft Office-compatible spreadsheet and word processing software. Cell phone photos can be saved online, which eliminates the need to store the pictures on a local computer. Some contact management applications are online-based. This allows you access to your files wherever you are, but you will need connectivity other than Wi-Fi to have constant access to your files. If you intend to purchase a tablet, make sure it has an affordable data network plan. Check to make sure that any device has Bluetooth connectivity, which allows you to communicate wirelessly with other Bluetooth devices such as printers and cell phones.

Cell Phone

You don't need to have the latest and greatest phone in order to be productive. Carriers pick different phones to support, so unless you're paying more to buy an unlocked phone, which is not restricted to a particular phone company's service, the individual contract options and costs may dictate the phone you purchase. However, the phone's operating system may also play a part in your decision. If you use Outlook for your email, calendar and contacts, Android phones won't sync with local, non-Microsoft Exchange applications. You can read your Outlook email, but you can't sync calendars or contacts unless you are using Google's online calendar and contact database and sync the phone's data with them. You can pay additional money for a sync app, but Blackberry and Window phones allow the user to sync with Outlook for free. Technology evolves and this situation may improve over time, but check the phone's specifications if it's important to you. Bluetooth connectivity allows you to wear a wireless earpiece.

Camera

Every real estate professional needs a digital camera. Real estate pictures don't require high-resolution settings, so five megapixels are more than adequate. The camera on your cell phone may suffice if it has zoom and flash capability. Check the specifications. Buy a camera with Bluetooth if you want to wirelessly transfer photos to your computer.

Printer

A Bluetooth-enabled laser printer allows you to print from your wireless devices. If your printer didn't come with Bluetooth functionality, you may be able to buy a USB Bluetooth adapter as long as the printer has a USB connector port. Check with the printer's manufacturer. Otherwise, you may be able to use an Ethernet cable that connects the printer to a router. If you are buying a new printer, make sure it has some type of wireless connectivity if want to maximize the use of your devices.

Document Scanner

Commercial real estate transactions tend to generate more paperwork than residential deals, and you want to store most of the information online and link it to your contact management database. If you have not yet purchased a scanner, and you think that you might want to store your documents online, or you plan to use a tablet as your primary computing device check to make sure that your desired model is compatible with "cloud" storage software. Cloud technology is the term used to describe applications that facilitate the use of online storage rather than on a computer's hard drive. Be aware that there may be privacy and security issues that need to be addressed, and that the storage space may cost you extra money.

Financial Calculator

The HP 10BII financial calculator is the standard for real estate analysis and the one that's used in this text's example problems. You can download the app or there's an interactive simulator available online at the following website that you can save to your computer, unzip the files and use to solve the course example problems.

> Website: http://www.educalc.net/1268086.page

Spreadsheet

Spreadsheet software is available from Microsoft (Excel), free Google Docs online shareable spreadsheet or Apple (iWork). Any of these will suffice. Advanced financial analyses use spreadsheets, and financial templates are provided in some commercial real estate courses. Other templates may be available in the public domain for a small fee.

Contact and Property Database

The contact management software may be the most expensive tool you'll need to purchase. It's also called customer relationship management (crm) software. You want an application that allows you to build an inventory of properties in your area of specialization and farm area. The software should allow you to enter property details, notes and associate contacts with a particular transaction. If property photos can be directly loaded into the application, that's a plus. If you want to easily access the data from any computer, you need to purchase a Web-based package. This gives you the most user flexibility, but you may have to pay for the online storage space. New products are introduced all the time, so do an Internet search for "commercial real estate crm software" to find the current offerings. Ask your broker for advice on what to purchase; your office may have a license for an application that qualifies for discounted pricing. Two of the popular currently available programs that include a contact and property database are highlighted below. You might want to participate in a free trial and try both applications and decide through hands-on experience, which works best for you. There are many other contact management tools without a property database, but if you buy a stand-alone package rather than an integrated one, you'll eventually need to purchase and learn a second piece of software.

- Real Estate Assistant (REA)

    REA has been in business since 1984 and was created by commercial real estate brokers who needed a way to keep their data organized. The program is designed around properties, and contacts are connected to properties as well as projects. This allows you to access everyone connected with a transaction by clicking on one button. Emails and files can be attached to a project and photos of the property are linked to the record.

    > Website: http://www.gorea.com

- REALHOUND

    REALHOUND has been assisting commercial real estate professionals since 1996. The powerful program is similar to REA in that both applications focus on properties. Unlike REA, REALHOUND users must renew the license annually. The application and data are accessed online.

    > Website: http://www.realhound.com

Step 2: Defining Your Market

Once you have the tools you need, it's time to get down to business. You've decided you want to specialize in commercial real estate, but the idea of it may be overwhelming you. Therefore, you need to narrow your focus to make your goal a manageable one. First, decide where you want to work and then decide what type of commercial real estate is most appealing to you.

I. Geography

Real estate professionals spend a lot of time driving buyers to view properties and driving to locations to talk to property owners. If you spend the majority of your time on the road, you're not being as productive as you could be. Unless you live in a rural area, you should not be driving more than an hour to look at properties. Residential real estate agents can make a living by selling homes in a particular subdivision or condominium; this is their "farm" area. There are fewer commercial properties than residential homes, so your farm area is apt to be larger than a few blocks. However, time is money so keep the distance within the one-hour driving time. If your chosen area is close to where you live or work, you will start to notice the properties as you drive by them. That's a good thing and helps you develop the expertise to become the "go to" person in your marketplace.

> **TIP: The better defined your geographic market place, the more effective you will be.**

II. Product Specialization

Unless you are extremely talented or live in an area where there are not a lot of commercial properties, you can't be all things to all people. It takes time to develop expertise in a particular property type. If you spread yourself too thin, you'll lose your effectiveness. This is one industry where being a "Jack of all trades" doesn't pay off. The basic types of products are office buildings, retail stores, apartments or multi-family buildings, industrial, and hotels and motels. Pick a type that personally appeals to you and one that is prevalent in your farm area. You might really like the idea of selling warehouses, but if the closest warehouses are two hours away, this wouldn't be a smart choice.

Office

Office property is one of the most common and recognized property types in the world. Offices come in a variety of different shapes and sizes ranging from the converted house to the high-rise office tower. Garden style offices are usually one- or two-story buildings arranged in a campus-like setting. Most garden-style properties are located in the suburbs while high-rise buildings are generally found in the Central Business District (CBD). Offices have been a preferred choice of investors for years. Property managers prefer long-term leases because the tenants are typically clean and don't usually destroy the property.

Buildings are often separated into classes that are based on the property's age, location, amenities and overall desirability.

- Class "A" Buildings

    A class "A" building is the latest and greatest building in the market place. It will generally have amenities like a marble lobby, atrium entrance, high-speed elevators, polished wood elevator cabs, valet parking, covered parking garage and the best location. However, class "A" varies with local market conditions and customs. In a suburban market, an "A" building may be a two story garden-style building; in New York City, the Empire State Building is old and is still considered an "A" class building. By the book, a class "A" office building is a high-rise building that is less than five years old with premium quality materials and finishes and located in the CBD of a 24 hour city.

- Class "B" Buildings

    A class "B" building is generally older than a class "A" building, less well-appointed and suffers from functional obsolescence; it has a style or features that are no longer in vogue. It isn't as desirable as a class "A" building. Functionally, it may have been an "A" building in the past but has now lost its appeal. It could have developed any number of unattractive characteristics including dated architectural style, tired interior finishes, a changed neighborhood, or the CBD may have moved. A "B" class building isn't a bad building; it's just a little less desirable than a class "A" property and commands lower rents. However, a "B" class building can be a very good investment opportunity. In times of economic uncertainty, many companies want to save money and prefer a well located and well maintained "B" building over a more expensive class "A" building. It's also possible for the owner of the "B" building to make improvements that appeal to tenants thereby turning it into an "A" building.

- Class "C" Buildings

    You've probably already guessed that a class "C" building is older and less desirable than a class "B" building. It may have been an "A" building at one time in the past and simply gotten older and maybe a little tired. A "C" building can become an "A" or "B" building by making improvements. The Empire State Building is old, but it's continuously updated and cleaned and maintains its class "A" building status.

- Class "D" Buildings

    Commercial real estate practitioners dispute whether a class "D" building actually exists. However, if you see a building that's off the beaten path (secondary or tertiary market), it's old, needs repairs and looks worn out, you could probably consider this a "D" class building. Many of these buildings have been chopped-up into small suites that are leased to start-up companies at a low rent rate. A "D" building can usually not be brought up to a class "A" or "B" due to its age and functional obsolescence.

Retail

A retail building comes in many varieties; there's the local nail salon and the national franchise store. The stores can be freestanding structures or part of a neighborhood or community center, a regional or super-regional mall, or a boutique. The one thing they all have in common is that somebody sells something out of them. Retail centers are typically anchored by a national or regional tenant. Grocery stores and drug stores are common anchors and appear at opposite ends of a neighborhood center. Sandwiched in-between the anchors are the smaller shops that benefit from the foot traffic that's created by the anchors.

Apartments/Multi-Family

Apartments and multi-family buildings represent another aspect of the real estate investment arena. For the purposes of this commercial real estate text, an apartment building consists of more than four units. Anything less than this is considered a single-family dwelling. Apartments come in a vast array of shapes, styles and configurations. Garden style apartments are generally two-story walkups in a campus type setting. High-rise apartment buildings can be found populating the center of most large metropolitan areas. There are converted large single-family homes and purpose-built buildings with hundreds of units. Old factories can be converted to lofts. Sizes of apartments range from a small efficiency to a penthouse with several thousand square feet, a private elevator and a rooftop pool. Most of the apartments you encounter are likely to be in the one bedroom/one bathroom to three bedrooms/two bathrooms range. All apartments and multi-family properties have the common feature of potentially producing a steady stream of income for their owners. One good aspect of the multi-family market is that people will always need a place to live.

Industrial

Industrial is also called warehouse property and comes in a wide variety of shapes, sizes and construction types. They range in size from the self-storage locker to giant manufacturing and distribution facilities. The building can be any height, have truck wells, rail sidings, barge mooring and tank farms. The facilities are often located in industrial parks, which are located near major highways, railroads, airports or seaports that can accommodate heavy traffic and shipping.

Warehouses can be freestanding or part of a greater whole; they can also be condominiums, which are shared by a number of tenants. There's virtually no limit to the number of uses for an industrial building. They can be built for a particular purpose such as a steel plant, or be built on spec to take advantage of prevailing market conditions. Industrial buildings are constructed from concrete block, brick, steel, tilt-slab or a combination of one or more construction types. Industrial transactions are larger and require a greater capital outlay than most other types of real estate investment.

Hotels, Motels and Special Purpose Properties

Hotels and motels are real estate, but due to the highly specialized nature of their operation, an in-depth discussion is outside the scope of this text. Hotels and motels, particularly the larger "flagged" properties, can represent a huge investment and sales opportunity. However, calculation of its value is different from other types of real estate investments. The hotel operates as an ongoing business concern and income is not derived from tenants, but it rather comes in the form of nightly rentals and ancillary services such as conference room rentals and restaurant and bar receipts.

Mobile home parks also fit into the category of special purpose properties. The investor buys the park and rents the pads to potential tenants. The park owner may offer other fee-based services such as rental of the clubhouse, utilities, management and rental services, laundry facilities and an on-site convenience store.

Another special purpose property type that may interest you is self-storage facilities. The warehouse is built and then subdivided into smaller units, which range in size from the classic 5' x 5' to more than 10' x 20'. These spaces are generally used for storage of personal goods, excess inventory or an overflow of office supplies or materials. The self-storage lease is usually a one-year term and is paid monthly by the party storing their goods.

As you can see, there is a wide variety of property types, and the key is to become a student of your chosen specialty.

TIP: You must know what it cost to build, own and operate your chosen property type. You must understand a tenant's cost associated with leasing a particular type of property.

III. Drive Your Market

Once you have decided what type of property most appeals to you, and you have defined your farm area, you need to drive through the area on a regular basis. That's one advantage to having your market area close to your home or office; you don't have to go out of your way in order to stay in touch with what's happening in the neighborhoods. As you are driving, pay particular attention to the changes in traffic flow and road closures. Road construction can have a severely negative impact on local businesses. Street widening projects tear up sidewalks so that both vehicular and pedestrian traffic slows; nobody's making any money if customers can't reach the stores or restaurants. Make it a habit to stop and talk to local merchants in your area. Pay attention to rumors that may affect your clients. For example, you may hear that an anchor store is leaving the center. Some leases may allow the other merchants to break their leases if the anchor leaves. If you are working with a potential buyer or tenant, this type of information is critical for them to know. That center may empty out quickly after the anchor leaves, and it may take a significant amount of time to recover. Your warning could save the client's neck and earn you future referrals from the grateful investor.

IV. Develop a Property Database

If you decide to buy a contact management system that contains a property database, it will simplify your life. Two of these products, REA and REALHOUND, were mentioned in the first chapter. It's strongly suggested that you purchase one of these or a similar product. Otherwise, you need to use two applications: one for contact management and one for property records. If you just want to get started and worry about buying software later, you can access the free online Google spreadsheets at docs.google.com; create an account if you don't already have one. The important thing is to start while you're motivated. Creating the property records for all the property in your product type is time consuming. Break the work into manageable chunks of time when you plan your daily agenda. Remember to plan your work and work your plan. Persevere and you will be rewarded.

Property Record

The first step is to find the properties by searching the tax records; it's much faster than driving around in your car. You'll look at the properties later when you take photos. The property search is most easily accomplished through the Multiple Listing Service (MLS). Search the tax records and enter the city and property use code for your farm area. The use code defines the property type for the search (multi-family, industrial, retail, etc.) and is most likely available as a drop-down-box selection. If it's not available, then hop in your car and find a property of your product type, enter the address of that property and use that use code in future searches.

This information is your starting point, and you need to enter all the relevant information in your software. Every property has a unique folio number or property id field; this is your unique identifier for each record and should be the first column in a spreadsheet or entered into your database software. Additional information that should be collected includes the street address, owner's name, phone number and address, year built, purchase date, size, number of units, square footage, land area, construction type, number of floors, number of tenants, whether it has docks, truck wells, laundry facilities, high speed elevators, types of finishes and any other special features. You might be able to find past or current listings that will supply some of that information.

Your database will be your "bank account" in commercial investment real estate. By building your database correctly from the start, you will be putting in an enormous amount of time and effort. Think of the process as a series of deposits; you are making daily deposits in your future income stream. Every time you complete a record or add another property to your database, you are depositing income into your career account. You are investing in your career; it's your future so please take the time to do it right.

Identify the Owners

If the tax record indicates that the owner is a corporation, you'll need to dig a little deeper. Go to your state's Department of State or Department of Corporations website and look up the name and address of the corporate officers. Data sources tend to be inaccurate 20 percent of the time, but you need to try to locate the phone numbers for the senior officers. One more accurate service that you might want to try is available from Argali and allows a free 30 day trial. For $29.95 a year, you have unlimited name searches, and both phone numbers and emails are retrieved. If the owner is a corporation, you'll need to make your calls to the President or Chairman of the Board because they are the ones with the decision-making authority.

> Website: http://argali.com

Photographs

Once you know where you're going, you can start to take photographs of every single property in your database. You will need the photos eventually when you do a proposal but, more importantly, it's critical that you know what you're talking about when you call an owner.

If you are working a product like industrial, it's a good idea to get as many pictures of the facility as you can. You'll want a picture of the front of the building, any unusual aspect of the building and any amenities such as truck wells, loading docks, generators or rail sidings. If you are working apartments, pictures of the pool, tennis court, clubhouse or any other amenities would be helpful. For retail properties, you'll want one or two photos of the entrance to the center, the anchor stores, any out parcels and anything else that makes the property interesting. If your specialty is office buildings, you'll want a front view and maybe several side elevations. If there is a parking garage or structure, you'll want a picture of that as well. You'll also want good pictures of the streets into and out of the property.

If you are storing your photos on your computer, put them in a folder labeled with the name of the folio identification number. This is the unique property identifier, which helps to keep you organized. You don't need to save the photos in their maximum size. If you don't know how to reduce the resolution, email them to yourself and choose the small size option.

V. Listing Sites

You may be able to find additional information on a property from past or current listings. The first place to search is your MLS and see if it shows up there. However, unlike residential listings, commercial listings often bypass the MLS and are entered in alternate sites. One reason why this is the case, is that the MLS requires that the cooperating broker is offered a commission, and commercial sellers may not be willing to do this. Therefore, alternative sites are used to list properties. That's one reason why you should always have a prospective buyer sign a Cooperating Broker's Agreement (see Appendix II). Among other things, that agreement allows you to contractually bind a buyer to pay your commission if a seller doesn't. Access the following websites for possible supplemental property information.

- Regional MLS
- CommercialSource.com
- LoopNet.com
- CoStar.com
- Commrex.com
- CityFeet.com
- Real-Buzz.com

VI. Organizations

Once you decide on your product type, you may want to join an organization that supports practitioners in that specialty. The group may hold national meetings, provide webinars and podcasts, publish newsletters, confer designations and certifications, and provide expert advice to newcomers in the field. The groups exist to help you grow your business. You don't have to join anything today, but you should be aware of the type of networking and educational opportunities that are available to you. Visiting these websites will help you understand what the initials after someone's name on a business card actually means, and it's an easy way to gain an insight into the type of training your competition feels is important. If you are interviewing with brokers, spending a few minutes on the sites is a fast way of obtaining an overview of the profession and may lead to a new position that's perfect for you.

National Association of REALTORS® (NAR)

Although the largest majority of NAR members specialize in single-family residential sales and leasing, there is strong support for commercial practitioners. The website has a designated commercial section, and additional useful information is found throughout the site. Your local Realtor association may have a separate membership program for commercial brokers and sales associates. Many of the local chapters also hold seminars on how to get started in commercial real estate that's geared toward the residential specialist. Check out your state and local association for additional information.

> Website: http://www.realtor.org/commercial

Building Owners and Managers Association (BOMA) International

This is an international organization, which was founded in 1907. There are over 16,500 members who specialize in building management and leasing. BOMA is an excellent source of information on building codes, building management and operations, leasing, technology, vacancy rates, building operating costs and legislation. Free articles are available on the website. Contact your local chapter of BOMA for membership information.

> Website: http://www.boma.org

International Council of Shopping Centers (ICSC)

The goal of ICSC is to help shopping center specialists develop their business. This is accomplished through networking, seminars, international meetings and research publications. Members can access a global directory of shopping centers that lists center name and location, owners' names, size, age, major tenants and contracts. Free newsletters are available on the website.

> Website: http://www.icsc.org

The Urban Land Institute (ULI)

ULI is a non-profit international organization with over 30,000 members who are interested in developing or redeveloping neighborhoods, communities and business districts. ULI sets the standards in urban planning. The magazine is available for free on their website. ULI offers a wide variety of professional development courses.

> Website: http://www.uli.org

The Institute of Real Estate Management (IREM)

IREM has approximately 18,000 members who are involved in managing all types of real estate properties, including multifamily. There are a large number of courses for members who wish to receive one of the recognized designations. A bimonthly magazine is available online for free on the website.

> Website: http://www.irem.org

Society of Industrial and Office REALTORS® (SIOR)

As the name indicates, SIOR is an organization for commercial specialists in the industrial and office segments. Members can complete course programs and attain professional designations. The online version of the quarterly magazine is free on the website. This international association has over 3,000 members.

> Website: http://www.sior.com

Commercial Real Estate Development Association (NAIOP)

NAIOP is another commercial real estate networking and education provider. This organization has over 15,000 members who specialize in industrial, office and mixed-use property types. Its members are also active in the area of government legislation as it affects real estate and the professionals who work in the field. Their quarterly online magazine is available on the website.

> Website: http://www.naiop.org

CCIM Institute

The CCIM Institute has an educational program that is suitable for all commercial real estate professionals. The classes provide advanced training in financial analysis, leasing and marketing. The student receives the prestigious Certified Commercial Investment Member (CCIM) designation when coursework, exams and required volume of transactions have been completed. The bimonthly magazine is available for free on the website.

Website: http://www.ccim.com

The REALTORS® Land Institute

If land sales interest you, this organization offers networking, referral and educational opportunities to its members. The association is for professionals who work with all types of land including agricultural, timber, recreational, farmland and special-use properties. For more information, visit the website.

Website: http://www.rliland.com

The Counselors of Real Estate

The Counselors of Real Estate is an international network of individuals who advise clients on complex real estate transactions. The group publishes a magazine three times a year, and it's available for a free download. Members must be invited to join the network, although this invitation can be self-initiated.

Website: http://www.cre.org

VII. Suggested Reading and Market Reports

The following list includes a series of links to incredibly valuable websites. If you're not sure what type of property you want to specialize in, these sites give you an insight into how that section of the industry operates and whether it is currently doing well or in the doldrums. Some of the sites may require you to register online in order to have access to the information. That's not a problem; go ahead and register.

- http://www.realtor.org/field-guides#topice

- http://www.realtor.org/reports/commercial-real-estate-market-outlook

- http://www.realtor.org/research-and-statistics/research-reports/commercial-real-estate

- http://www.cbre.com/EN/research/Pages/globalreports.aspx

- http://www.grubb-ellis.com/Research

- http://www.marcusmillichap.com/Services/Research/

- http://www.ccim.com/cire-magazine

- http://www.naiglobal.com/mr.aspx

- http://www.irr.com/Publication-PublicationList/Index.htm

- http://www.reis.com/index.cfm

- http://www.globest.com/

- Rackham, N. (1988). *Spin Selling*. New York: McGraw-Hill Education.

Step 3: Making the Cold Call

Most sales people hate the idea of making cold calls, but the idea of it may be worse than actually doing it. Once you do a few, you can get into the rhythm, and the sales pitch starts to sound more natural and less forced. You may or may not agree with that statement, but let's assume you're willing to try. Whom do you call? The answer to this rhetorical question is that the owners in your property database are one of your best sources of leads and an excellent place to start. These property owners may be in the market to buy or sell, and your objective is to establish a relationship with them. You do that by talking to them. As far as cold calling goes, the one and only reason to get on the telephone is to get an appointment. Everything you do in this initial contact phase is geared toward getting in front of someone with decision-making authority and establishing rapport. So, relax and follow the suggestions presented in this chapter and watch your business start to grow. Remember to persevere and plan your daily agenda.

I.   Word Emphasis

It's not what you say; it's how you say it. You've probably heard that before, but it bears repeating. The emphasis that you put on certain words can totally change the meaning of what you are saying. Take a minute to look at the following examples.

I did not say he took the money.   (I didn't say it...but somebody else did.)

I **did** not say he took the money.   (I didn't say it...though I may have implied it.)

I did **not** say he took the money.   (I didn't say it...at all...so leave me out of it.)

I did not **say** he took the money.   (Again...I didn't say it...hint...hint.)

I did not say **he** took the money.   (He didn't take it...but somebody else sure did.)

I did not say he **took** the money.   (He simply borrowed it...unauthorized...of course.)

I did not say he took **the** money.   (He didn't take the money...he took other money.)

I did not say he took the **money**.   (He didn't take the money...but he took everything else.)

Do you see how a simple change in emphasis can totally change the entire meaning of the sentence? The words themselves didn't change, just the meaning.

II. Voice Inflection

Inflection refers to the pitch of your voice. We've all had phone calls from monotone, robotic telemarketers whose droning voice and mispronounced words lead to quick hang-ups. Don't let this be you. You should practice what you're going to say and role play with a friend before you call your first prospect. In particular, you want to avoid elevating the pitch of your voice after you introduce yourself.

For example, if you say "Hi Bob, this is John Doe, and I'm from XYZ Realty" and your voice trails up at the end of the sentence, you are apt to get an unwanted reaction from the prospect. Don't be surprised if you hear "I've never heard of you. Why are you calling me?" This is not the desired response.

When you elevate the pitch of your voice, you're actually asking a question. Whether or not that's your intention, that simple act of elevating the pitch conveys that you're unsure about what you're doing or saying. It gives the party you're calling the opportunity to exit the call.

III. Psychological Captivators

To use a fishing analogy: the purpose of the cold call is to attract the fish, dangle the bait, set the hook and reel it in. The method to accomplish this is by using the four psychological captivators, which are known in the advertising world as AIDA (Attention, Interest, Decision and Action).

Attention

When you want to get the attention of someone, call him by his first name. In "How to Win Friends and Influence Enemies," Dale Carnegie wrote, "Remember that a man's name is the sweetest and most important sound in any language." Think about it. When a telemarketer calls and asks for Mr./Mrs./Ms. [insert your name here], you're immediately aware that the person doesn't know you. However, if someone calls and says, "Hi, [insert your first name here]," you try to figure out who is calling and don't instantly lose interest.

> TIP: Always use the prospect's first name when you're cold calling.

Interest

Once you have your prospect's attention, you need to dangle the bait and talk about something that will interest him. If his name is in your property database, then you already know he's an investor, and investors are interested in money. One of the following topics may entice your prey:

- How to make more money (yield)

- How to make more money, quicker (term)

- How much it will cost them (investment)

Of course, there are other things you could talk about, but these three topics are likely to be at the top of the list for most investors. The real estate market varies from area to area and from time to time so you need to try to keep current with the prevailing market conditions. At the end of this chapter, there are scripts that you can adapt to meet your needs.

Decision

You need to be talking with someone who has the authority to make decisions regarding the sale or purchase of real estate. If the owner of a property is a corporation, locate the name and contact phone number for the president or chairman of the board. Once you've confirmed that you're speaking to the proper person, and he is still on the phone after your initial presentation, then the time has come to set the hook before he gets away.

Suggest a meeting and see what happens. You can say something like "So what I would like to do is to take a look at your building and see if it makes any sense for you to even consider selling." The seller will now say that it makes sense, and you should get together, or he'll say it doesn't make sense and there's no reason to meet.

If the call doesn't result in an appointment, go on to the next. If that call isn't productive either, go on to the next. Every time you get knocked down, get back up. You don't have to like it; you just have to do it. The more calls you make, the better you'll get. The better you get, the more appointments you'll get, and appointments are the very lifeblood of the business.

Action

You managed to get the investor's attention; he's interested, and he's decided that it's worth his time to meet with you. Now it's time to firm up the appointment commitment and reel him in.

Remember that you're not trying to sell anything over the phone. You are only looking for an opportunity to meet with him, and you may need to steer the conversation in this direction.

The sellers may not have read this book and simply will not follow the game plan. In fact, they may ask you questions like "What do you think my building is worth?" or "How much do you charge?" or any number of other prickly questions. The best way to handle this is to not answer. Turn the conversation back toward setting a time for the appointment.

Seller: "How much do you think my building is worth?"

Sales Associate: "It depends on a number of factors. What I really need to do is to take a look at your building and do my homework. When would be a good time for us to get together?"

Notice that the sales associate did not lose sight of the objective, which was to get the appointment to meet the owner face to face at the subject property. Once you have a meeting of the minds, you can get the commitment.

Sales Associate: "Bob, do you have a calendar there? Great, pencil me in for [appointed day and hour]. Let me give you my cell phone number in case anything comes up. See you [appointed day and hour]. Thank you."

Bingo! Now you've got them hook, line and sinker. By getting them involved in the process, they are buying into the appointment and have made a commitment.

Remember: The Four Psychological Captivators	
A	Attention
I	Interest
D	Decision
A	Action

IV. Discussion Topics

There are many possible topics that you can employ to break the ice during the cold call. The one thing you never want to ask is "How are you?" That's apt to lead the discussion in a direction you never intended to go and one that may be hard to reverse. Talk about property, financing or new legislation; choose something that will pique the interest of an investor. Brainstorm with your broker or mentor for ideas. Meanwhile, feel free to use the following ideas and accompanying scripts. After a while, you'll develop your own style and discover what works best for you. You need to get over your fear of failure and just start dialing. Practice makes perfect, and you will learn from your mistakes.

Just Listed

Whenever you get a new listing, call everyone in your property database to see if they know anyone who might be interested in purchasing it. Who knows? They may even want another one for themselves.

Just Sold

When you sell a property, call everyone in your database to check if they know anyone who might be interested in selling. Tell them you have a list of prospective buyers, and they may decide to sell one of their own investments.

1031 Like-Kind Exchange

Many real estate professionals may be unfamiliar with exchanges. The good news is that many investors are also unaware of a 1031 Exchange. The 1031 Like-Kind Exchange portion of the IRS tax code permits an investor to defer indefinitely the payment of capital gains tax following the sale of investment property. It's a complicated provision, but the key components are that the seller never personally touches the proceeds of the sale, there are strict time constraints in which to act, and the entire amount of sale proceeds is reinvested in the purchase of one or more similar like-kind properties. For example, your investor could sell his warehouse and use the proceeds to buy an apartment building or a store or one of each if there are sufficient funds. Check out the 1031 tax code at http://www.irs.gov. Take some time to read the many additional articles on the Internet that help to explain all the variations of the code.

Depreciation

The IRS allows investors to deduct depreciation on a commercial property for the first 39 years of ownership. This is a calculated amount of straight line depreciation that is unrelated to the actual condition of the property. The depreciation reduces the amount of annual taxes owed by the investor. If you have saved the purchase date in your property database, accessing properties that have been owned for over 30 years is an easy task. Mention the benefits of depreciation as a tax shelter in your cold call. Combine this with the opportunity for them to defer capital gains tax by investing the proceeds of the sale into the purchase of another property via a 1031 exchange.

Hold Time

The average hold time for an investment property is around seven years, so if you include purchase dates in your property database, it should be an easy task to retrieve the relevant records. If property values have appreciated, contact all the owners who purchased their property more than seven years ago and mention the benefits of a 1031 exchange.

Balloon Mortgage

Someone who bought in the last 3-7 years could be a potential seller if he has a balloon mortgage payment coming due. The mortgage or deed of trust is recorded in public records, so include the loan information in your property database. The effectiveness of this technique depends on current interest rates and property value appreciation. If interest rates are higher, and property values have increased, they may prefer to sell before the loan balloon payment comes due. In this case, be sure to mention the benefits of a 1031 exchange. If interest rates have decreased and property values have stayed relatively constant, the owner may prefer to refinance the loan, rather than sell the property. If interest rates have decreased, and the value of the property has significantly increased, the investor may prefer a cash-out refinance; they pay off the balloon payment with a new mortgage and use the balance of this larger new loan to purchase another property. Cash-out money usually is not considered taxable income.

Sale-Leaseback

Another great target is a building that is owned by the company that is using the building. This makes very little sense; a business can't deduct the operating expenses of the building (real estate taxes, depreciation, insurance cost) from the operating income of the building.

A sale-leaseback is a transaction in which the business sells the building to an investor and enters into a long-term lease as a condition of the sale. The lease and sales price are based on current market conditions.

The investor gets to take all the deductions for operating the building as an investment property, they have a reliable tenant and a steady stream of income. The seller/lessee gets to deduct the lease as an operating expense; it's 100 percent tax deductible in this case. In addition, the seller gets a pile of cash to redeploy into the business.

To determine if a building is a likely candidate, you might have to visit the properties in your farm area to uncover whether or not the owner is using the building. However, if the address on the property deed matches the address of the owner, flag this in your property database as a sale-leaseback possibility.

> TIP: Always send a hand-addressed thank you note after a cold call and include your business card and a photograph of the property.

> TIP: If someone tells you to call them back in six months, call him back in three; cut the time in half or he may already be working with someone else.

> TIP: Always caution investors to contact their tax advisor before entering any real estate transaction.

V. Sample Scripts

Here are a few samples of cold call scripts. Modify them as you see fit.

Just Listed

Phone:	Ring, ring.
Seller:	"Hello."
Sales Associate:	"Hi Bob. This is John Doe of XYZ Realty, and the reason I'm calling is we just put the property at 123 Payton Place on the market. Now, I'm not calling to ask you if you want to buy it. But, I know you own a building in the neighborhood, and I was wondering if you had a friend, supplier or associate who may have told you they wanted to be in the area. Who should I let know about this property?"
Seller:	"Well, nobody comes to mind."
Sales Associate:	"Bob, while I've got you on the phone, I have to ask the question. Would you be interested in the property?"
Seller:	"Nope, I'm all set."
Sales Associate:	"Thanks for taking the time to speak with me. I'll keep you posted."

Just Sold

Phone:	Ring, ring.
Seller:	"Hello."
Sales Associate:	"Hi Bob. This is John Doe of XYZ Realty, and the reason I'm calling is we recently sold the building at 123 Payton Place. As a result of our marketing campaign we have had a number of buyers who came late to the table. What I'm hoping is that you know of somebody in the area that was thinking of making a change. Maybe a neighbor, supplier or friend, and we could get them together and make something happen."
Seller:	"Nope, nobody comes to mind."
Sales Associate:	"Bob, Thanks for taking the time to talk to me. If you hear of anything, would you give me a ring?"
Seller:	"Sure, why not?"
Sales Associate:	"Great, let me give you my number. It's 954-555-5555. Thanks again. Goodbye."

1031 Tax Deferred Exchange

Phone:	Ring, ring.
Seller:	"Hello."
Sales Associate:	"Hello Bob. This is John Doe of XYZ Realty, and the reason I'm calling is we are currently working with a buyer who is involved in a 1031 tax-deferred exchange. What I'm hoping is that you have a friend, supplier or maybe someone you do business with that is thinking about making a change."
Seller:	"Hmmm, nobody comes to mind."
Sales Associate:	"Bob, it sounds like you might have something in mind."
Seller:	"Well, now that you mention it, we could use some more space."
Sales Associate:	"Well, let's get together and take a look at your building and see if we can help you."
Seller:	"Ok."
Sales Associate:	"Take a look at your calendar. Pencil me in for _____. Just in case something comes up, let me leave you my cell number."

> TIP: Whenever you hear the hmmm in a conversation, it should alert you that the other person has something else on his mind, and it's time to do a little digging.

Step 4: Keeping the First Appointment

The first appointment is your big opportunity to impress the client with your real estate acumen. If you do it right, 70-80 percent of the real work is completed during this step. The first appointment is where you begin the proposal process that includes the gathering of information and the definition of the seller's problem. During the first appointment, one of two things can happen: you'll spend time building rapport and then return at a later time to gather documentation, or you'll determine that the client has an immediate need and collect the necessary data during your first visit. If you have an unsuccessful meeting, you'll go home a little bit older and a little bit wiser. Learn from your mistakes and do it differently the next time.

I. The Business Development Call

The business development call is the type of first appointment where you become acquainted with the client, put a face to the voice and leave without any supporting paperwork. You are simply there as a public relations gesture; trying to establish rapport and begin building a relationship with the client. What do you think the possibility is that a person who has never met you before would be willing to offer up all the relevant information regarding the leasing, management and operations of their property? If the client has something in mind, then the scenario may change in your favor. You have a valuable service to offer, and they may make the decision to let you into their little world.

A true business development call will typically last approximately one hour and should include a rapport-building segment, a brief introduction of yourself and your company, and an interview to see what strategy, if any, the client has regarding their property.

Rapport

You want to establish a common ground between you and your client. This will come much more easily for the gregarious person than the shy one, but everyone can do it. You need to talk about something your prospect finds interesting. FORM is an acronym that may help you come up with ideas; it stands for Family, Occupation, Recreation and Money. Dale Carnegie once wrote, "You can make more friends in two months by becoming interested in other people than you can in two years by trying to get other people interested in you."

However, don't fake it. Don't do it unless you are genuinely interested in the other person. Your client will recognize the insincerity, and it will blow up on you. The bottom line is that you'll lose.

However, don't despair; listening attentively is a trait you can develop. Look around the office and look for clues to the client's interests. Pictures on the desk or wall can act as conversation starters, and displayed trophies and awards can also help to break the ice. Let FORM show you the way.

- **Family**. If you notice pictures of children, say something like "That sure is a lot of children." The client may then come back with "Those are all my grandchildren; all 10 of them." You can then inquire if his children live locally, and that may lead to a 30 minute discussion of his kids. Listen to what the person is saying and ask questions to keep the conversation flowing. Remember, if you see family pictures, it's probably an indication that the owner of the photos would be happy to talk about them.

- **Occupation**. During the course of your career, you will meet people from many different walks of life. If an investor has an unusual job, ask them about it, or perhaps the owner of a company doesn't match the usual stereotype. For example, a female owner of a machine tool manufacturing plant probably has an interesting story of how she got into a male-dominated business. Ask her and see if it induces her to talk about her start in the industry. If not, move on to another subject.

- **Recreation**. Do you see anything on the desk or wall that indicates an interest in a particular sport? Maybe there's a signed football in a place of honor on a bookshelf. There might be a golf trophy on the desk or a sailfish mounted on the wall. Whatever catches your eye is a possible conversation starter. If you know nothing about football, but you are an avid fisherman, ask about the sailfish. Stay interested and ask questions. It's easier than you may think.

- **Money**. Investors are in the business of making money and are usually interested in hearing about anything that may have a positive or negative impact on their ability to make more money. Maybe interest rates are going up, or rent rates are going down, or there is talk about possible changes to the capital gains tax laws. Stay current with events that are happening in the financial markets, and you may find yourself with an attention-getting conversation starter. Remember to let the investor do most of the talking. Talking about money may segue into a discussion of politics, which is an inflammatory subject that you want to avoid if you hold opposing views. Keep the conversation going in a productive direction.

Remember: FORM
F Family
O Occupation
R Recreation
M Money

Client Assessment

Once you've spent about 30 minutes establishing rapport, it's time to move on to the next step. At this point, the focus of the conversation should shift to an assessment of the investor's needs. Listen carefully and take notes during this portion of the conversation. This accomplishes a couple of things; it impresses upon your client that you genuinely care about their needs, and it gives you the opportunity to ask follow up questions. INVEST (Intent, Needs, Verify, Executive, Services, Teamwork) is an acronym to help you remember what topics to cover during the assessment phase.

- **Intent**. The first thing you need to determine is what your investor intends to do. Although you have already gleaned some information from your initial phone call when you made the appointment, there are still important details to uncover. For example, on the phone he may have told you that he's selling his building; now you need to follow up and determine if he's planning to use the proceeds to buy a different property. If that's the case, find out what kind of property he is interested in buying.

- **Needs**. Before you can find a solution, you need to define the needs. At this point you know if he intends to buy or sell, now dig a little deeper and find out why. What is his motivation? Why does he need to do what he's doing? It's your job to help the client find the best solution to his problem.

  If he's moving because his manufacturing business is expanding due to a new contract, you might ask a question like "Mr. Client, what does that additional business mean to you? What does it mean to the company? What would it mean to you or the company if you did not meet your deadline and couldn't deliver on the contract?" He could reply that the contract is worth millions, and it could be the difference between our contact having a job or not the next time we call back. That simple question is providing you with the key to selling the client. If you present a solution that not only satisfies the client's need but also helps them succeed, it's no longer selling; you have become a trusted advisor. Fascinatingly enough, the client may actually ask you what you think they should do. There is a huge difference between trying to cram something down a client's throat and having him ask you to help him acquire the space.

  Perhaps he's planning to sell because he needs money, but you know that the market is currently flooded with similar properties, and that he won't get the price he's looking for. In a case like this, if interest rates are low, and he has sufficient equity in the property to make a cash-out refinance a possibility, you might suggest he wait until it's more of a seller's market. You lose the sale, but you'll probably get future business from him, and meanwhile you gain a reputation as a trusted advisor. A true sales professional will recognize when there is a genuine need and will not attempt to sell, manipulate, cajole, coerce, influence, maneuver, direct or otherwise influence a sale when one is not needed.

In addition to his motivation for investing, you have to determine his timeframe. Commercial transactions can take much longer than what might be expected. The buyer has a right to have the property and the books inspected, and there may be proposed tenant improvements that have to be approved. The attorneys will draw up, review and revise the written offer. All of this takes time. Add the time it takes to move-in and set up furniture and equipment, and you could be looking at months of prep work. You have to let the naive investor know what to expect from the process. If he tells you he needs to move within an unrealistic amount of time, you might be wise to walk away. Otherwise, steel yourself because you're in for a bumpy ride.

Finally, try to determine if the stated space requirements are reasonable. If the company is moving from one facility to another because it needs to expand, look at the current location and do your own estimate of required additional floor space. If the company is on a growth spurt, it may need more space for future expansion that the owner hasn't taken into account. Listen to your client and take careful notes.

- **Verify**. Before you agree to help someone, you have to verify that he has the financial resources and requisite experience to do what he plans on doing. Ask your client what resources he has budgeted for the move or acquisition. Successful investors get that way because they care about costs and the expected return on their investment. If someone tells you "Money's no object," it's because they have no money. However, if the client has a realistic budget, you may decide to move forward and help satisfy his real estate needs.

    Before you move too quickly, there's one other piece of information you may need to verify. If your client is planning to buy a property and lease the space to tenants, a lender may require proof that he has previous property management experience. For example, funding may be difficult to obtain if the client plans to buy an office building with 50 suites, and he has no prior experience with tenants or property maintenance. Ask your client for his resume and email it to your trusted lender or loan originator before you decide to commit yourself to the project. Find out if his expectations are reasonable. Instead of an office building, he might want to improve his profile and purchase a few duplexes. Once he has the management experience, he can move on to a larger property.

- **Executive**. If things are going well, and you feel comfortable pursuing the client, ask him if someone else who needs to be involved in the decision-making process. An investor may want to include a significant other, and if the client is a corporation, you may need to have the approval of the chief executive or board of directors. You want to avoid having to duplicate your efforts. If you're going to make a formal presentation, you want all the decision makers to be in the room. That may not be possible, but it's your goal.

- **Services**. This is the part of the discussion where you distinguish yourself from your competitors. If you're just starting out, stress the qualifications of your brokerage firm. If the firm is new to commercial real estate, talk about your education and familiarity with the neighborhood. Maybe discuss various ways you might list and market the property. One of the best ways to begin a conversation about how you are different is to ask the client about prior experiences he may have had with other real estate brokers and sales associates. Listen attentively and don't interrupt. When he's done, never denigrate another company or real estate professional; you'll look petty or sleazy. Instead, say something like "You know Mr. Seller, traditionally you'd be right. Brokerages used to work that way. Let me tell you how we operate, and I think you'll see a substantial difference." If the client has been unhappy with a prior lack of communication, say "Every Friday I will send you an email telling you what I have done to market your property." If you say it, be sure you do it. If you perform, word will spread like wildfire in the community. You'll win more business simply by delivering what you promised. If you want to get famous, deliver more than you promise and watch what happens.

- **Teamwork**. Once you complete your assessment of the client's needs and abilities, and you decide that you want to proceed, you need to get the client's buy-in. You may approve of him, but the reverse may not be true. How do you find out? You ask by saying something like "If we can agree on price and terms, is there any reason you can think of for not using us?" If he replies with "Uh...hmmm...well..not really," take that as a warning and stop. Anything that follows that type of hesitation is usually a lie. Be on guard. However, if he thinks you're great, then you can start working together as a team.

Remember: INVEST	
I	Intent
N	Needs
V	Verify
E	Executive
S	Services
T	Teamwork

II. Data Collection

Data collection is the second phase of a first appointment. You want the information so that you can determine a reasonable list price for a property. If your introductory phone call went extremely well, you may have already emailed him a list of what you need. Otherwise, follow him to the office and wait while he goes through his files, or you can set a time when you can come back and retrieve the requested information.

You need to document the building's income and expenses, and verify the owner's mortgage terms and loan balance. To make your job easier, you can use the First Appointment Checklist on the next page and modify it to suit your needs. You will need the information that you collect to prepare the listing proposal, which is covered in the next chapter.

First Appointment Checklist

In order to perform the most complete analysis of your property to ensure the highest possible price for you, it is imperative that we have as much information as possible regarding the property. It has been our experience that problems don't jeopardize transactions-surprises do. It makes it much easier to not only get you an "At-List" offer, but to close the transaction with the highest net proceeds to you.

1. One year of rental receipts or a copy of the ledger.

2. Receipts for the past 12 months of repairs, maintenance, utilities and landscaping.

3. Tenant lease agreements.

4. Service contracts.

5. The mortgage and note documents.

6. Recent mortgage statements.

7. Accounting of escrowed funds.

8. Partnership agreement if there are co-owner partners.

9. Any other relevant details.

Step 5: Preparing the Listing Proposal

At this point in the process, you have not yet secured the listing. You've established rapport, determined needs and verbally agreed to work together as a team, but that's very different from having a legally binding listing agreement. Typically, a listing agreement isn't signed until the seller decides on a list price, and you want that price based on facts and not emotion. Commercial real estate determination of value is usually more complicated than taking the average of the adjusted sale price of recently closed comparable properties, which is the standard method used by residential real estate sales associates to generate the Comparative Market Analysis.

Commercial investors are interested in the income stream generated by the property, and many owners are also concerned with the potential for future profits gained by selling the property after an appropriate holding period. They want to maximize the return on their investment. The purpose of this section isn't to make you a financial wizard; there are specialty courses you can take that focus on investment property analysis. However, you will need a financial calculator to follow along with some of the examples.

This material explains some common financial concepts and gives you enough information to get started. Some investors throw around terms, which they may not fully understand, and may ask you to determine a list price based on any of the measures presented in this chapter. Similarly, buyers often request that you find them properties that meet certain financial criteria. If you study this chapter, you'll at least understand what they want, and you might even be able to suggest a better approach.

I. Supporting Material

Before you start crunching numbers, there's some preliminary research work to do. When you present your proposal, your audience wants to understand how their property compares to similar properties in the area.

Data

In order for you to do a listing proposal, you must gather a great deal of information. The previous chapter included a checklist form letter and now is the time to organize the documents you've received from the seller. You must have a copy of the leases that affect the property, the utility bills and the annual operating statement indicating all expenses related to the operations of the building. In addition, you need to know the current debt service, whether or not the mortgage is assumable, and the amount of any prepayment penalty. You also need any maintenance contracts and contracts for services such as lawn care, elevator care and janitorial. You can translate the meaning of the zoning code by using the following website.

> Website: http://www.municode.com/Library

Photographs

You need photographs of the property to make your presentation pop, to use when you post your listing on the Internet and to refresh your memory. As time goes by, and you get busier, the salient features of the property may be harder to recall. Take lots of photos and go back and occasionally look at them. You'll need pictures of the property's interior, exterior, special features, parking structure, curb cuts, signage, and ingress and egress.

Comparables

Finally, you have to gather information about comparable sales that are closed sales on properties that are similar in style, size, configuration, age, utility and location to the subject property. In real estate lingo, a subject property is the one that is being appraised or otherwise evaluated; in this case, it's your seller's property, and you are trying to determine its market value. You need to document the sale price and rent rates for these closed sales.

You'll also need to gather information on the competition and take exterior photographs of any listed comparable properties. In addition, you'll need to get rental information on the other area properties that are for sale. Find out the following things:

- Terms of the lease.

- Do the competing buildings offer free rent or tenant build-out?

- Is parking included or do the tenants have to pay for it?

- As consideration for the tenant entering into a lease, will the landlord offer a moving allowance and pay for new stationary and the cost of moving computer and telephone equipment?

If all the other property owners are offering generous terms, you want to know this information to help determine a list price, and it will be useful when you're trying to procure a buyer for the property. A new owner is likely going to have to offer similar terms as the competition if he wants to lease the units in a timely fashion.

II. Annual Operating Statement

The seller will provide you with a copy of the annual operating statement, but that data may be incorrect or incomplete. Therefore, you need to re-create it from the building's income and expense information you collected from the seller in the previous step and from your research on competing properties. First, you'll learn the different components of an operating statement, and then you'll be given a formula and design that you can input into a spreadsheet and use as a template for your future transactions. All figures are based on annual calculations, and the end goal is to determine the annual income cash flow, both before and after the mortgage payments.

Potential Gross Income (PGI)

Potential gross income is all the income a property would produce if it were fully leased. However, when you're working with commercial properties, there are two types of rent to consider: contract rent and market rent. Contract rent is what the tenant agrees to pay in the lease, and that's what you should use when evaluating office, industrial and retail properties that generally have long-term leases that are in effect for 3, 5, 7 or even 10 years.

Market rent is the rent that's customarily paid in the marketplace and is most commonly associated with apartment rentals. Tenants usually rent apartments for a year or less, so the prudent real estate associate will use the current rate in the formula to calculate actual cash flow and repeat the calculations using market rent. That way, if the current rent is less than market rent, the marketing material can publish actual cash flow as well as mention projected increases in cash flow if the new owner raises rents when the leases terminate.

> **TIP: Include any common area maintenance fees (CAM) paid by tenants in the PGI**

Vacancy and Collection Losses

Always include a factor for vacancy and collection losses. Even if the seller tells you that the property is rented 100 percent of the time, that's an aberration that can't be maintained. Tenants leave in the middle of the night; checks bounce, and vacancies may take a few days or weeks to fill. Many analyst use a set value of 7 percent of the PGI for the vacancy rate. Actual numbers for your area and property can be obtained by subscribing to REIS's services, or you can obtain free reports from Integra Realty Resources.

> Website: http://www.reis.com
> Website: http://www.irr.com/Publication-Publication_MarketSnapshot/Index.htm

Additional Income (AI)

Additional income can come from a number of sources including laundry rooms, vending machines, parking fees, cable charges, greens fees, clubhouse rental, forfeited rents, late fees and bad check charges. Always look for additional income when reconstructing an operating statement because it can represent a large portion of the annual income, which subsequently increases the value of the property.

Effective Gross Income (EGI)

Effective gross income is the normalized income that's adjusted for vacancy and collection losses and includes additional income. It's the amount of generated money that the owner uses to pay the operating expenses and the mortgage. Hopefully, he winds up with a little bit of a return at the end of the day. Our cash flow formula at this point is:

PGI *minus* (.07 *times* PGI) *plus* AI *equals* EGI.

So far so good. This concludes the income portion of the operating statement; let's proceed to a discussion of expenses.

Operating Expenses (OE)

Operating expenses are the expenses that the owner incurs in the operations of the building. They are unrelated to the type of business; the building expenses should be similar no matter who is occupying it. Of course, manufacturing and business office suites will have dramatically different utility charges, but they won't be residing in the same type of buildings. Advertising charges, business cards and personal income tax are all business expenses, not operating expenses, and don't belong in this section. This will be the largest section on your spreadsheet template.

There are three types of operating expenses: fixed expenses, variable expenses and reserves. Fixed expenses are those expenses associated with the operation of the building that don't vary with tenancy; property tax and property insurance are two examples. The cost of variable expenses depends on the number of tenants using the services; for example, the bills for water, sewer and electricity increase depending on usage.

Reserves for replacements is the last type of operating expense; you can think of it as a forced savings account. It's an allocation of money set aside in a separate bank account to replace capital items such as roofs, air-conditioning units, parking lots and other large items that have measurable life expectancies. For example, if a particular type of roof is expected to last 15 years, and it was new 10 years ago, you know that you'll have to replace it in 5 years or so. The reserve account allows the owner to prepare for expected replacements and build up the kitty over time rather than being unexpectedly hit with a major future replacement bill. Reserves are not included in the operating expense section of the spreadsheet and don't affect the seller's published net operating income. Fixed and variable operating expenses are deducted from effective gross income, which yields the net operating income. The formulas for cash flow are now complete.

PGI *minus* (.07 *times* PGI) *plus* AI *equals* EGI   AND   EGI *minus* OE *equals* NOI

As a general rule of thumb, operating expenses typically range between 35-85 percent of EGI. Older buildings usually require greater reserves for replacements than brand new buildings of the same type.

TIP: Always include a management fee of 3-6 percent to operating expenses.

Net Operating Income (NOI)

The net operating income is the income that the owner has left over after paying the building expenses and before he makes the mortgage payment. Owners want this income stream to be as large as possible because it's directly related to the investment value of the building. The more income the property nets, the more attractive it is to potential buyers.

One way of increasing the NOI is to pass along the cost of utilities to the tenant. In the case of apartment buildings and other full-service buildings, the landlord can install separate water or electric meters for each tenant. That forces the tenant to pay for their own utilities; thereby reducing the building's operating expenses, which increases the amount of NOI. The following page is a spreadsheet template for reconstructing an operating statement. Modify it to suit an individual property; you're likely to need additional or different operating expenses.

Reconstructed Operating Statement

Property Name _____

Location _____

Type of Property _____

Annual Mortgage Payment _____

POTENTIAL GROSS INCOME _____

    Less Vacancy and Collection Loss _____

    Plus Additional Income _____

EFFECTIVE GROSS INCOME _____

Operating Expenses

    Real Estate Property Taxes _____

    Property Insurance _____

    Utilities:

        Water _____

        Electric _____

        Gas _____

        Sewer _____

        Trash Removal _____

    Accounting and Legal _____

    Licenses and Permits _____

    Building Advertising _____

    Building Supplies _____

    Off-Site Management _____

    Payroll _____

    Employee Benefits _____

    Taxes/Worker Compensation _____

    Miscellaneous Contract Services:

        Elevator Maintenance _____

        Landscaping _____

        Pest Extermination _____

TOTAL OPERATING EXPENSES _____

NET OPERATING INCOME _____

    Less Mortgage Payment _____

    Less Funded Reserves _____

CASH FLOW BEFORE TAXES _____

III. Financial Analysis Overview

Now that you have collected the property data, you can start to analyze what you have and determine the investment value of the property. This is different than market value because it's based on the concept of investment returns. While you can use the calculations to derive a reasonable list price or offer amount, every investor is unique with different investment goals. Some may want a large monthly positive cash flow; others may be satisfied with breaking even every month as long as the property value appreciates. The one common goal is that everyone wants to make money. However, the desired rate of return varies among individuals.

You want to be in a position to answer questions about the income potential of a property. If you're the listing agent, you'll include the numbers in the listing. Some investors will understand them, and some won't. But now you'll be in the driver's seat and can explain the potential under a number of different scenarios. You can also help buyers to realize the full potential of their investment. Just because they can afford to buy a commercial property, doesn't mean they are investment experts. You can help.

The rest of this chapter covers the following most common measures of return:

- GRM — Gross Rent Multiplier
- GIM — Gross Income Multiplier
- Cap Rate — Capitalization Rate
- Cash on Cash Return — Cash Flow before taxes
- IRR — Internal Rate of Return
- PV — Present Value
- NPV — Net Present Value
- FMRR — Financial Management Rate of Return

IV. Multipliers

Multipliers are based on property income without taking the building expenses into consideration. It's a simple technique, and multipliers can be a reflection of an investor's needs, or they can be market-derived. Multipliers come in two forms: gross rent multiplier and gross income multiplier. The two are frequently used interchangeably; however, the gross rent multiplier is based solely on monthly rental income, while the gross income multiplier is based on annual lease income and includes other funds collected from the tenants for amenities such as parking, vending machines or laundry facilities.

Gross Rent Multiplier (GRM)

Monthly Rent x Desired Return = Value

Suppose that your investor tells you that he wants to buy the property at 80 times the monthly rent. Eighty is the GRM. If the total monthly rent is $5,000, the investor is willing to offer $400,000.

$5,000 x 80 GRM = $400,000

Gross Income Multiplier (GIM)

GIM measures the ratio between the amount of money a property takes in on an annual basis and what "return" is required by the investor. If we know both of these factors, we can determine a reasonable offer price.

Annual Gross Income x Desired Return = Value

If the property generates $120,000 a year, and your investor tells you he wants to buy it at 9 times gross income, the offer price should be $1,080,000.

$120,000 x 9 GIM = $1,080,000.

Calculating Market Rates

You've just seen that an investor may stipulate a return rate, but multipliers can be derived by analyzing rents for recently sold properties within a neighborhood. Search the MLS to gather the required information.

You now know that Monthly Rental x GRM = Sale Price; the related formula is therefore

Sale Price ÷ Monthly Rental = GRM

Comparables	Sale Price	÷ Monthly Rental	= GRM
1	$300,000	$2,000	150.0
2	$280,000	$2,000	140.0
3	$350,000	$2,400	145.8
4	$290,000	$1,900	152.6
5	$320,000	$2,000	160.0
Totals			748.4
Neighborhood GRM = 748.4 ÷ 5 comparables = 149.68			

If you have been following this example, it's easy to see that the neighborhood market-derived GRM is 149.68. Therefore, if you have an investor who's interested in making an offer on a property with a monthly rental income of $1900, a fair offer for the property is:

$1,900 x 149.68 GRM = $284,392

Limitations of Multipliers

Both GRM and GIM are easy investment measures to use, but they are both extremely limited in utility. The primary limitations are:

- GRM and GIM make no provisions for operating expenses. The property could be the proverbial "money pit" eating the owner alive, and there's no recognition of that in either measure.

- GRM and GIM don't take mortgage payments into account.

- GRM and GIM make no consideration for income tax, and the tax-sheltering benefits provided by owning investment property.

- GRM and GIM make no provision for multiple years of ownership and accrued appreciation.

V.   Cap Rate

Cap rate is real estate lingo for capitalization rate, which is usually defined as either the investor's desired rate of return on investment or the market rate of return. However, as you proceed through this chapter, you will see that this is an oversimplification. Cap rate is simply the relationship between the net operating income and the purchase price.

IRV Formula

For our purposes: I = annual net operating income (NOI)
R = cap rate
V = value of the investment

If you know the value for two of the factors, you can calculate the third.

$I = R \times V \qquad V = I \div R \qquad R = I \div V$

Use the following drawing to help you remember. I equals R times V; cover the V and you have $I \div R$; cover the R and you have $I \div V$.

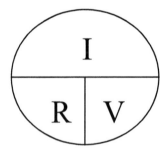

Suppose NOI is $40,000 and the investor wants an 8 percent cap rate. Plug in the numbers to calculate the value.

V = I ÷ R   V = 40,000 ÷ 08   Solving for V, the value equals $500,000

You can use this as the starting point for an initial offer on the property.

Now suppose the NOI is $35,000 and the list price is $600,000. What is the cap rate?

R = I ÷ V   R = 35,000 ÷ 600,000   The cap rate in this example is 6 percent.

If the investor wants a higher return on his investment, one of two things needs to change; either the NOI increases or he pays less for the property. For example, he decides to offer $500,000 for the property. What is the cap rate now?

R = 35,000 ÷ 500,000   The cap rate now is 7 percent.

Alternatively, the rents are below market, and the investor believes he can increase the NOI by raising the rents when the leases are renewed. If the projected NOI is now $45,000 a year and the list price is still $600,000, the cap rent increases.

R = 45,000 ÷ 600,000   The cap rate is now 8 percent.

One more example should help clarify any remaining confusion. If the investor wants a 10 percent rate of return and the list price is $450,000, what is the NOI?

I = R times V   I = .10 x 450,000   I = $45,000

Remember the formula that's used to calculate annual NOI, which is the property's cash flow before the mortgage or income tax payments are made.

	PGI (Potential Gross Income - annual)
minus	Vacancy and collection losses
plus	Additional income (vending machines, parking, washer and dryer)
equals	EGI (Effective Gross Income - annual)
minus	Operating Expenses
equals	NOI (Net Operating Income - annual)

Using Market Cap Rate When Listing a Property

Once you have reconstructed the operating statement, you know the annual NOI. You need to calculate an estimate of the property value, but you don't know what cap rate to use in the IRV formula. You can find an average cap rate for your area and property type by subscribing to REIS services, or from Integra Realty Resources free of charge. Note that these are the same two sources that provide vacancy rates by area and property type.

> Website: http://www.reis.com
>
> Website: http://www.irr.com/Publication-Publication_MarketSnapshot/Index.htm

You can obtain more specific information from the MLS which usually includes the NOI in the listing. Search for recently sold properties of similar size, style, configuration, age and location and calculate the cap rate based on sale price: R = NOI/sale price.

Once you have calculated the market cap rate for similar closed sales, solve for value and use that number as the list price in your listing presentation:

Take a look at the following example.

Comparables	Annual NOI	÷	Sale Price	=	Cap Rate
1	$36,000		$350,000		.103
2	$38,000		$370,000		.103
3	$41,000		$420,000		.098
4	$35,000		$380,000		.092
5	$38,000		$330,000		.115
Totals	$188,000		$1,850,000		.511 ÷ 5
Market Cap Rate : Use IRV	$188,000 ÷ $1,850,000 = .102		OR average		.511 ÷ 5 = .102

You can either add the comparables' total NOI and divide by total sale price or calculate the cap rate for each property, add them up and divide the total by the number of comparables. You get the same answer either way, although there may be rounding differences. The calculations result in a market cap rate of 10.2 percent, which you can round down to 10 percent.

If your seller's property has an NOI of $39,000, the estimate of market value is:

$V = I \div R$ $V = 39,000 \div .10$ which is $390,000

Limitations of Cap Rate

Cap rate is the relationship between the net operating income and the purchase price. Nothing more and nothing less. However, you will meet with investors who will tell you that they want a specific cap rate. Use that as a starting point in your discussions. You need to know the whole picture and convey that information to your investor.

For example, suppose a building is half empty and is listed at a 2 percent cap rate. Would your buyer consider it? Probably not. But, you find out that next month a major national tenant is starting a 20 year lease. That certainly changes things and your buyer might reconsider his initial rejection.

Now look at the flip side. A building is listed at a 12 percent cap rate, and your buyer can't purchase it fast enough. However, you find out that the anchor tenant who occupies 70 percent of the building is leaving next month. That also changes the picture and not in a good way.

TIP: Verify all leases.

Cap rate takes into account building expenses but doesn't address the following issues:

- Cap rate doesn't take mortgage payments into account.

- Cap rate doesn't make any consideration for income tax, and the tax-sheltering benefits provided by owning investment property.

- Cap rate doesn't make any provision for multiple years of ownership and accrued appreciation.

VI. Cash on Cash Return

The Cash on Cash Return measures the return on the cash (initial investment) used to acquire the investment against the pre-tax cash flow. In simpler terms, it compares your investment to your cash flow after the mortgage payment (debt service).

The Cash on Cash Return can often be referred to as your Return on Equity (ROE) or Return on Investment (ROI), but it should never be referred to as a return on your down payment. The down payment and your initial investment can be substantially different. The down payment is the amount of equity required by the lender as the buyer's contribution to the transaction. The initial investment includes the down payment, closing costs, inspection fees, mortgage application fees, points, and any other capital additions made at the point of sale.

Let's look at an example. You may be surprised to discover that financing a purchase increases an investor's rate of return. There's more to life than a cap rate.

	Potential Gross Income	$100,000.00
minus	Vacancy & Collections Losses	- $5,000.00
plus	Other Income	+ $0.00
equals	Effective Gross Income	$95,000.00
minus	Operating Expenses	- $45,000.00
equals	Net Operating Income	$50,000.00
minus	Debt Service	- $32,000.00
equals	Cash Throw Off	$18,000.00

If the investor wants a 10 percent cap rate, he'll make an offer of $500,000 for the property.

$V = I \div R$ $V = 50,000 \div .10$ which is $500,000

Okay, so far so good. This should look familiar. Now let's suppose that the buyer wants to obtain a mortgage from a commercial lender, and that he qualifies for a loan at 80 percent LTV. LTV means Loan-to-Value, and it's an indication of the amount of money the lender will loan. In this case, the offer is $500,000 and the lender is willing to loan 80 percent of that amount, which is $400,000. The total purchase price is $500,000; the lender will finance $400,000, so that leaves $100,000 that the investor must bring to the table as a down payment.

Now let's go one step further and assume that the interest rate on the loan is 8%. To keep it simple, assume that this is an interest-only loan. If that's the case, the annual mortgage payment is:

$400,000 x .08 = $32,000.00

Subtract the $32,000 debt service from the $50,000 NOI and you get an annual Cash Throw Off (CTO) of $18,000.

Rate of Return

The CTO is the cash investors get to keep after they make their mortgage payment. In a very real sense, the tenants in the building are actually paying the mortgage for the investors so the CTO represents a return on their investment. The initial investment is the $100,000 down payment plus closing costs. Assume that the closing costs are $15,000. The CTO represents a return on those funds. To establish the rate of return, take the CTO and divide it by the initial investment to get a rate.

Cash Throw Off ÷ Initial Investment = Cash on Cash Return (ROI)

$18,000 ÷ $115,000 = 0.16 or a 16 percent return.

Not bad. The Cash on Cash return is a whopping 16 percent. How did that happen? If you bought the property at a 10 percent cap rate, how did you end up with a ROI that exceeds the cap rate? The answer is leverage, and this example is a classic illustration of positive leverage; the use of other people's money to obtain a higher rate of return. Leverage is covered in more detail later in the book.

Limitations of Cash On Cash Return

- Cash On Cash Return doesn't make any consideration for income tax, and the tax-sheltering benefits provided by owning investment property.

- Cash On Cash Return doesn't make any provision for multiple years of ownership and accrued appreciation.

The ROI takes into account building expenses, unlike GRM and GIM. It also considers the debt service, unlike cap rate. There is a place for Cash on Cash Return as an investment measure, but there is something better, more sophisticated and certainly more informative. Read on!

VII. Financial Calculator

In the first chapter, you were directed to purchase the HP 10BII financial calculator. If you haven't had time to do this yet, download the app or there's a simulator available online at the following website that you can download.

Website: http://www.educalc.net/1268086.page

The HP 10BII financial calculator user manual is located at the following website. If you have time, read the Introduction and the first chapter to familiarize yourself with the calculator keys. When you're ready, you can read Chapters 4-6 in the manual that explain cash flow calculations. These three chapters are chock full of valuable, easy-to-read information and clear illustrations. If you don't have a computer or calculator handy, just follow along for now and try to understand the concepts. You can repeat the rest of this chapter when you're prepared.

Website: http://h10032.www1.hp.com/ctg/Manual/bpia5213.pdf

If you choose not to read the manual at this time, go to Appendix IV for a quick tutorial on using the HP 10BII financial calculator. The next two sections in this chapter will be easier to understand if you are comfortable with the calculator.

VIII. Internal Rate of Return

The Internal Rate of Return (IRR) measures the expected rate of return on an investment that is held over a period of time; you're making money on money. It's called an internal rate because it's not dependent on interest rates or inflation. In addition, for our purposes, you will expect to sell the property (reversion) for a profit at a later time. What is your total expected IRR? Hint: Expect it to be greater than the cap rate or cash on cash return.

Let's use the previous example. You buy a property for $500,000 with a $400,000 loan, $100,000 down, $15,000 closing costs, and you expect to get a positive cash flow of $18,000 per year. Now assume you can sell the property in 5 years for $700,000. Don't worry about how to project the amount of appreciation that far into the future. What is the IRR?

It may help you to draw a diagram to visualize the problem.

Year	0	1	2	3	4	5
Pay-Out	-$115,000	$18,000	$18,000	$18,000	$18,000	$18,000 + $300,000

Every financial analysis transaction needs money coming in and money going out. The initial investment of $115,000 is negative because it's money going out of your pocket. The $300,000 in year 5 reflects the proceeds of the sale. The loan was interest-only, so the loan payoff is $400,000, and the projected future sale price is $700,000. The difference between these two numbers is $300,000.

Enter the following key strokes into your calculator to calculate the IRR.

Key	Purpose
0 FV	Clear the value
0 PV	Clear the value
0 PMT	Clear the value
0 I/YR	Clear the value
1 Gold Key P/YR	Number of payments per year. P/YR is under PMT on top row
115,000 +/- PV	The Present Value is -115,000. The +/- key is left column, 4th row from top
18,000 PMT	Yearly payout
300,000 FV	Future Value is profit from resale
5 N	5 Payouts
I/YR	? Requesting rate of return - press this key
Displays	32.58%

The expected Internal Rate of Return is 32.58%, and all your investor wanted was a 10% cap rate. How did this happen? Well, leverage had a little to do with it, but the major factor was the influence that the reversion had on the investment. The investor bought the property for $500,000 and sold it for $700,000 just five years later. Plus, the property generated a good positive cash flow during the hold period.

Limitations of Internal Rate of Return

- How do you know you can sell the property for that amount 5, 7 or 10 years in the future?

- Is the IRR a pre-tax or post-tax return?

This text is not going to go into any depth regarding the tax implications of real estate ownership, and the tax shelter associated with the ownership and disposition of the property. However, do yourself a favor and read about IRS Section 1031 Like-Kind Exchanges that allows an investor to defer paying capital gains indefinitely; there's a lot of information available on the Internet.

IX.   Present Value and Net Present Value

Present Value (PV) and Net Present Value (NPV) are ways of assessing what a stream of future income is worth in today's dollars. Suppose you won a prize that was going to pay you $100,000 every year for the next 10 years. That's great, but you decide that you want a lump sum payment now rather than collect it in chunks over 10 years. What is this annuity worth to an investor if you want to sell it? Hint: it will be less than the total $1,000,000 income stream because annuities sell at a discounted rate.

Decision-Making Factors

Investment value is different for every individual. If you were contemplating buying an investment with a multi-year income stream, what would you be willing to pay for it? There are many types of investments including real estate, stocks, bonds, mutual funds, antiques and collectibles. What factors are apt to affect your decision?

- Inflation

    Inflation has an insidious way of eroding the value or purchasing power of money. It causes money to lose its ability to buy goods or services. There are many theories about what inflation is, but we can all agree that the cost of many things keeps going up; that's inflation.

- Opportunity Cost

    Opportunity cost is the cost associated with being denied the use of your money. If you lend or invest your cash today, you have less cash to take advantage of an opportunity that comes your way. So, shouldn't you be compensated for the lost opportunity; shouldn't you get a return that satisfies you for the missed opportunity today?

- Risk

There are many kinds of risk; financial risk, insurable risk and non-insurable risk, but the one you're concerned with is risk of capital. The very real possibility that the money you invest may not come back to you in the near future, or that it may not come back at all, which is default risk. When you invest your money, wouldn't you like to know you're going to get it back? How many people would invest in a given instrument if it were guaranteed not to return their investment? Not a whole lot.

- Taxes

There may be ways to shelter the income, but for all practical purposes investment income, which is the return on your money, is fully taxable.

Rate of Return

Risk is related to interest rates as well as rates of return. Investors buying certificates of deposit (CDs) are protected by the FDIC and will not lose money on their investment, within federally regulated limits. Bonds are riskier than CDs but less risky than real estate. Real estate is probably riskier than investing in blue chip companies, but real estate in poor locations or condition is riskier than prime real estate. High-yield junk bonds have the highest return, but are the riskiest investment. For this exercise, assume the following given rates of returns.

- CDs - 3%

- Government Bonds - 4%

- Blue Chip Corporate Bonds - 7%

- High Yield Bonds - 17%

Real estate generally falls in the middle of the range and has value even if it's not fully leased or occupied. Remember that under every single building there is land that adds some residual value to the real estate. The other thing about real estate is that there are any number of possible alternatives in which to invest, and some leases even require the tenant to pay for all the maintenance, insurance, utilities and property tax on the building.

In constructing a rate of return, you want to get enough money to compete with a reasonably comparable investment. You want to make sure that inflation doesn't eat you alive, and you probably prefer to have the yield cover the taxes associated with the return on your investment. Now, this isn't a scientific or even economic discussion, and the setting of rates differs from investor to investor. In addition, there are other factors to consider such as the source of capital and if any promises have been made regarding guaranteed yields. The intent of the following example is just to illustrate a yield for discussion purposes.

Present Value

Suppose you want an investment that returns a little more than U.S. bonds (4%), keeps pace with inflation (2%) and compensates for income taxes (3%). Add up the numbers, and it looks like you're willing to accept a 9% return on your money. If that's the case, what are you willing to pay for an investment that generates $100,000 income stream every year for 10 years and returns 9% on the investment?

Year	0	1	2	3	4	5
Pay-Out	?	$100,000	$100,000	$100,000	$100,000	$100,000

Year	6	7	8	9	10	
Pay-Out	$100,000	$100,000	$100,000	$100,000	$100,000	

You want to know what to pay today for a future income stream. This is an example of Present Value. Using your HP 10BII calculator, enter the following keys.

Key	Purpose
0 FV	Clear the value
0 PV	Clear the value
0 PMT	Clear the value
0 I/YR	Clear the value
1 Gold Key P/YR	Number of payments per year. P/YR is under PMT on top row
10 N	10 payouts
9 I/YR	Investor's desired rate of return
100,000 PMT	Payment
PV	? Requesting Present Value - press this key
Displays	- 641,765.77

The answer is - $641,765.77 Remember, money that you pay is negative; money you receive is positive.

Net Present Value

Net Present Value analyzes an offering price against the income at an investor-desired rate of return. Suppose that you have the same income stream of $100,000 a year for 10 years, but now you want a 10 percent rate of return. The property is listed for $625,000. Does this price achieve your target yield of 10 percent?

If you haven't cleared the settings from the previous problem, just input:

10 I/YR
PV

The answer is -614,456.71. Consequently, you will not achieve your 10 percent return unless you offer $614,456.17, which is substantially less than the $625,000 list price.

So far in this chapter, all the periodic payments were for the same amount and occurred at regular intervals. If the payout varies, you must use the cash flow application on your calculator. The next example uses even cash flows to demonstrate another way to calculate NPV, but remember that it handles uneven payments as well.

Cash Flow Problems

In the CFj application the "j" indicates the group number; as you enter the 10 payments, the 1-10 group number is displayed. Here's the problem:

Year	0	1	2	3	4	5
Pay-Out	-625,000	$100,000	$100,000	$100,000	$100,000	$100,000

Year	6	7	8	9	10	NPV
Pay-Out	$100,000	$100,000	$100,000	$100,000	$100,000	?

Here is the sequence of key input:

Key	Purpose
0 FV	Clear the value
0 PV	Clear the value
0 PMT	Clear the value
0 I/YR	Clear the value
1 Gold Key P/YR	Number of payments per year. P/YR is under PMT on top row
625,000 +/- CFj	Initial investment is negative. The +/- key is left column, 4th row from top
100,000 CFj	Year 1 payment
100,000 CFj	Year 2 payment
100,000 CFj	Year 3 payment
100,000 CFj	Year 4 payment
100,000 CFj	Year 5 payment
100,000 CFj	Year 6 payment
100,000 CFj	Year 7 payment
100,000 CFj	Year 8 payment
100,000 CFj	Year 9 payment
100,000 CFj	Year 10 payment
10 I/YR	Investor desired rate of return
Gold Key NPV	Request NPV value. NPV is under PRC on second row
Display	-10,543.29
Gold Key C ALL	Clears the registers. The C ALL key is under C in the left column

The NPV result indicates that you must pay $10,543.29 less than the $625,000 list price if you want to achieve your desired 10 percent rate of return. The following key sequence can be used if there are multiple consecutive equal payments.

Key	Purpose
0 FV	Clear the value
0 PV	Clear the value
0 PMT	Clear the value
0 I/YR	Clear the value
1 Gold Key P/YR	Number of payments per year. P/YR is under PMT on top row
625,000 +/- CFj	Initial investment is negative. The +/- key is left column, 4th row from top
100,000 CFj	Year 1 payment
10 GOLD Key Nj	10 equal consecutive entries. The Nj key is below CFj.
10 I/YR	Investor desired rate of return
Gold Key NPV	Request NPV value. NPV is under PRC on second row
Display	-10,543.29
Gold Key C ALL	Clears the registers. The C ALL key is under C in the left column

By now, you should be getting the impression that there are as many different yield requirements and ways by which to calculate them, as there are investors looking for investments in the market place.

X. Financial Management Rate of Return

The Financial Management Rate of Return (FMRR) is an investment measure typically used only by institutional investors and bankers. An in-depth discussion is outside the scope of this course, but this type of analysis recognizes that there may be times of negative cash flow. For example, if extensive renovations are being planned at a future time, this methodology takes into account that the preceding cash throw off income stream can be invested in a safe interest-bearing account that will earn income to fund the deficit. Government bonds are a likely choice for reinvestment income. The reinvestment rate is a rate at which the cash flows will be reinvested in another investment and produce further yields outside the property.

This is one of the most complex but most accurate measures available because it considers taxes, mortgages, positive and negative cash flows, and the reinvestment of cash as it comes out of the investment.

XI. Additional Resources

This chapter isn't intended to turn you into an overnight expert. The CCIM Institute, on the other hand, specializes in classes that focus on commercial real estate investment analysis. The classes aren't cheap, but they are useful. You can start with the Introductory course which covers the basics of the HP 10BII financial calculator and investment analysis. If you're not too overwhelmed, and you have the resources, you can move on to the CCIM 101 course.

Website: http://www.ccim.com/course/catalog

Check out the following website for useful tools that cover the material presented in this chapter. The term APOD, which you'll see on the website, refers to the reconstructed operating statement that you learned about at the beginning of this chapter.

Website: http://www.garytharp.com/forms/

Step 6: Presenting the Listing Proposal

If you've been following the steps as they were laid out in this text, you must be feeling confident at this point. You've managed to build rapport with the seller, and you've collected as much information as possible about the property. The previous chapter showed you how to crunch the numbers to arrive at a reasonable list price. This chapter discusses the packaging and presentation of the proposal.

I.   Proposal Package

Your proposal needs to appeal to different types of personalities. Some sellers will want to know more about you, your company and past clients. Other owners will focus more on the property details and comparables. The following outline is just a suggestion; modify it as you see fit. You also might want to ask your broker if she has a template you can use before you start reinventing the wheel. Reiwise produces comprehensive and attractive listing proposals for a reasonable annual subscription fee. Take a look at some samples on the following website.

> Website: http://www.reiwise.com/ciaoSamples.aspx

Cover

The cover page should include a color photograph of the front of the property and perhaps a smaller one of the interior. The property name (if it has one) and address, your company name, address and contact information. In addition, your name and contact information should be neatly positioned on the page.

Table of Contents

An indented style works well for this page. Section names should be in a large bold font and left justified on the page. The individual components of the section look good in a smaller bold font indented under the section heading.

Introduction

The Introduction section contains an Overview subsection of what is contained in the presentation. It should contain a disclaimer that the data presented came from reliable sources and is believed, but not guaranteed, to be accurate. The Conditions subsection states that the presentation is prepared for the sellers and that the information it contains is confidential and shouldn't be released to a third party without your company's permission. If there are tenants in the building, you want to emphasize that you haven't talked to them to discuss their future intentions to renew their leases; your opinion of value is based on the current tenants and rents.

Qualifications

The Qualifications section presents an agent profile and a company profile. If the company is just beginning to become involved in commercial transactions, this will be a short section. However, if the agent or broker has completed some transactions, you can create a table that lists the name and address of the property, type of property, square footage and sales price. You might want to include a subsection that enumerates the reasons why the seller should list with you and not a competitor. This subsection may include things like integrity, familiarity with the market area, your marketing plan, and your willingness to provide continuous updates. The last topic to cover in this section is an explanation of how you will find and work with buyers. You can explain that you have a database of prospects (these are the owners of similar properties in the database) and that your marketing data is current and reflects an accurate valuation. You can assure your potential seller that you'll meet with the buyers in person to discuss the advantages of owning the property, and you'll create an environment that promotes buyers bidding against each other, which leads to a higher sales price.

Property Details

You are making the presentation to the sellers who know their own property, so this section is a summary that they can use to more easily compare their property with the comparables. Create a chart to contain the basic information: property name, address, legal description, assessor's parcel number, owner, year built, square footage, rent per square foot, size of lot, type of construction, type of roof, property amenities, tenant names, zoning, parking, type of financing and loan balance, and assessed value. You can include an aerial photograph if you have access to one.

Demographics

Location, location, location. That's a real estate mantra that holds true for residential as well as commercial properties. Many tenants are willing to pay higher rents for an attractive building in a well-maintained neighborhood. High-end professional service tenants may prefer to reside in a city where the population is well educated with high household incomes. On the other hand, a company that does strictly Internet business and doesn't have to meet with customers may not be willing to pay the higher premium commanded by an affluent location. Presenting the demographic summary to the sellers will help them to better understand the market. Your Realtor ® association may have tools you can use that allow you to download demographic information for areas surrounding the property. This could include average age of residents, education, income and racial composition of the area. Additional information can be found by conducting an Internet city-specific search; enter <city name> demographics and you may be able to retrieve a large number of full-color pie charts and tables. Right-click on an image to save it to your computer. The color graphics really make the report "pop."

Rent Comparables

This section should contain three subsections for leased properties that are similar to the seller in terms of size, type and location. The first subsection presents a color photograph and data for each comparable. The information should include the address and type of property, year built, rentable square footage, lease rate per square foot, common area maintenance (CAM) fees, and minimum required lease term and occupancy rate for each property. The second subsection organizes the information as a compact chart, and the third subsection is a map showing the location of all the rent comparables.

Sale Comparables

This section contains the same three subsections as the rent comparables, except that now you are using properties that have sold in the past six months. The data in the first subsection also changes. For this portion, you want address and type of property, sales price, year built, rentable square footage, price per square foot and closing date.

Pricing

The Pricing portion of your listing proposal summarizes all of your hard work from the previous chapter and contains five subsections. The following table is a summary of the information used to derive the calculated values in the first subsection's table.

Annual Gross Income	$100,000
Annual CAM Recapture Income	$61,900
Net Operating Income	$96,000
Cash Throw Off	$47,686
Rentable Area	5,002

- The first subsection presents the financial indicators. The formulas used to derive values are in the right column for demonstration purposes only. Don't include the formulas in an actual report.

Price	$1,000,000	
Down Payment	$250,000	
Pro Forma CAP	9.6%	$96,000 ÷ $1,000,000
Cost Per Sq. Ft.	$199.92	$1,000,000 ÷ 5,002
Average Rent Per Sq. Ft.	$19.92	$100,000 ÷ 5,002
CAM Per Sq. Ft.	$12.38	$61,900 ÷ 5,002
Cash on Cash Return	19%	$47,686 ÷ $250,000

- The second subsection contains a property abstract.

Type of Property	Retail
Type of Lease	NNN
Year Built	1975
Lot Size	12,000
Net Square Feet	5,002
Parking Spaces	15

- The third subsection displays the projected financing details. Look in Appendix IV - Exercise One for the sequence used to calculate mortgage payments using a financial calculator.

Loan Amount	$750,000
Interest Rate	5%
Loan Type	Fixed Rate
Term	360
Annual Payment	$48,314

- The fourth subsection summarizes the property's operating expenses. This is a NNN lease in which the tenant pays all utility costs.

Taxes	$20,400
Insurance	$5,000
Maintenance & Repair	$30,000
Utilities	$0
Management	$4,000
Physical Reserves	$2,500
Total Expenses	$61,900

- The fifth subsection displays the pro forma annual operating data for our hypothetical property.

Scheduled Gross Income	$100,000
Plus CAM Recapture	$61,900
Plus Additional Rents	$1,000
Total Income	$162,900
Less 5% Vacancy	($5,000)
Effective Gross Income	$157,900
Less Operating Expenses	($61,900)
Net Operating Income	$96,000
Less 1st Year Loan Payment	($48,314)
Pre-Tax Cash Flow	$47,686
Cash on Cash Return	19%

Marketing Plan

The marketing plan you present can be a couple of pages long or be more than 10. It depends on how verbose you want to be. If you make a template, you only have to create this once, and it can be used verbatim for every other listing presentation you produce in the future. Whatever you put here, make sure that you follow it. You can describe what you'll do on a week-by-week basis for the first four months or so. Another approach is to give a narrative account for the first four weeks and then use a bullet list for the following weeks. Typical entries will include sending the seller an update on activities, advertising on your website, calling prospective buyers in your database, sending postcards to prospective buyers, broadcasting the initial listing to multiple websites and placing ads in newspapers.

Disclaimer

You want to protect yourself by including a disclaimer in the footer of each page in the report. The wording should state that you believe the information is accurate, but you haven't verified it and make no guarantees or warranties as to its accuracy. Look at the bottom of an MLS listing to see a concrete example of a disclaimer that's there to protect the listing agent.

Now you have your proposal in hand, and you have distributed a copy to everyone in the room. You're standing tall, looking good and ready to present your sales pitch to the interested parties. But before you walk up to the podium; there's one more thing you need to consider. You have to tailor your presentation style to match the personality of your audience; otherwise, you risk losing the listing.

II. Personality Types

You don't need to be a psychologist in order to be a successful salesperson; however, a basic understanding of how different types of people make decisions may improve your chances for success. Research into personality types has been going on since Hippocrates (400 B.C.). One of the current and more popular theories was introduced by Dr. William Moulton Marston in 1928 and goes by the acronym DISC.

DISC Theory

The DISC theory postulates that people exhibit characteristics associated with one or more of the four possible personality descriptions: dominance, influence, compliance and steadiness. There may be overlapping traits, but these general descriptions allow you to anticipate an individual's actions. These four traits and associated behaviors can be displayed in a tabular format.

	Task-Oriented	*Relationship-Oriented*
Fast Decisions	**DOMINANCE**	**INFLUENCE**
Slow Decisions	**COMPLIANCE**	**STEADINESS**

Each cell in the table represents an intersection of two types of traits. For example, dominance describes task-oriented individuals who make decisions quickly, and steadiness applies to relationship-oriented people who need time to ponder a decision.

If you are observant during your first appointment with a client, you can gain considerable insight into their personality. Look at the office furnishings; family pictures or the lack of photos provides valuable clues. Notice style of dress and manner of speech. Pay attention, and it will help you later.

Dominance Characteristics

The Dominance characteristics include strong egos, decisiveness, efficiency, competitiveness, independence, being open to change and practicality. On the flip side, people who are strong in the dominance section of the DISC profile can also be tough, harsh, impatient, pushy and self-centered.

These people are very businesslike in their attire and demeanor. They arrange their office in an efficient manner and tend to make decisions rapidly; they are generally very decisive. They are task oriented; give them an assignment and they will complete it or die trying. These are going to be your classic "A" type personalities; the hard-boiled business people who run a company by sheer force of will.

They will want to know what an investment costs, when they'll get it and what it does. They like information fast and without frills and digression.

Influence Characteristics

People who fit the Influence personality categorization tend to be stylish and fashionable with the latest cool clothes and gadgets. Their workplace tends to be loaded with cool stuff, a little messy, cluttered and very personal.

Their pace is fast, and they tend to be spontaneous decision makers. They like interacting with their vendors and business associates. They are the guys and gals who do most of their business on the golf course or on the fishing boat.

They crave recognition and fear loss of prestige and face. They want to know how an investment will enhance their status, and who else uses your services; the more prestigious your clients are, the better they like it. They like recognition, compliments and acknowledgement. They want to be admired by subordinates and coworkers, and they value status in the workplace.

In order to gain their support, you need to support their ideas and goals. In turn, they will support your proposition.

Compliance Characteristics

The Compliance people are formal and conservative. They are structured, organized and thrive on functionality. This type of person is a slow, methodical decision maker who requires all the facts and figures. They are task oriented and are very much concerned with the "process." They prize accuracy and precision. They want to make and justify every decision purely on logic and fact. They are the Mr. Spocks of the world who want to know how a proposition works and how it will benefit them.

These individuals are prepared and expect you to be too. They seek precise answers so be ready to give them what they want. If something costs $475.16, don't round it off. Give them the full amount to the penny. Their primary concern is to preserve their credibility in the organization, and they value their own correctness and thoroughness above all else. They measure themselves by their precision, accuracy and activity, and they are deliberate to a fault. They will do anything to avoid embarrassment and a loss of credibility.

They want to know all the facts, and you will have to go through every page of your presentation and explain how you arrived at your numbers and conclusions.

Steadiness Characteristics

People who are strong in the Steadiness traits like a more casual and comfortable environment. They tend to dress casually and comfortably and generally conform to the prevailing dress code of the organization.

Their office will be populated with family pictures and keepsakes. There may be an overstuffed chair in the office accompanied by pictures of their pets. This type of individual thrives in a friendly, relaxed and informal environment.

Their decision-making process is slow and involves a great deal of soul searching. They will solicit the opinions of all their friends, family and coworkers; they may even consult a psychic. These people fear confrontation and strenuously seek to preserve relationships.

They will look at how your services will affect them personally and in the eyes of their company, coworkers and cohorts. They look to you to be pleasant. They want to be liked and are put off by people who are insensitive or inpatient.

III.   Presentation Style

You have to recognize that the listing presentation is not for your benefit. It's solely for the benefit of your clients, and you must learn to talk in terms of their needs, goals and aspirations. Some people want to know all the facts before they make a decision, and others just want to hear the salient points. You need to gauge the reaction of your audience and adjust accordingly.

Take a minute to go back and review the DISC table that was presented earlier in this chapter. The people with the greatest Dominance or Influence traits will make faster decisions than the Compliance and Steadiness types. The Dominance and Compliance individuals are task-oriented and want the facts, and they may not necessarily care about building a relationship with you. The Influence and Steadiness types will want to know more about you and your other clients.

If you met all the decision makers at the first appointment, then you should have a good idea of what to expect from them during the presentation. If you are meeting some of them for the first time, you need to pay attention to their body language and listen to what they are saying.

If the sellers aren't objecting to anything in your proposal, you might as well pack up and go home. You haven't engaged them, and they're not interested in what you're saying. On the other hand, if they object to the suggested list price, then you have interested sellers, and you want to work hard to make your case. Prove to them that you've done your research and know your market. Go get them! Snag the fish, sink the hook and reel them in.

Dominance Presentations

When you're dealing with Dominance individuals, you might want to ask them if they want the Reader's Digest Condensed Version or the long protracted version. They'll usually choose the condensed version because they want the facts without the fluff.

If they want the short version, turn directly to the price and terms sheet of the proposal and tell them something like "According to the market-derived data your property is worth $2 million dollars." Now sit back and watch what happens.

If they ask how you arrived at the price, show them. If they object, say, "Perhaps I overlooked something. What did I miss?" Then listen to their remarks because they are showing you that they are serious about selling the property.

Most people who are new to the business try to avoid discussing the price and terms in what they believe to be too rapid a fashion. This is a HUGE mistake. Dominant personalities like to make quick decisions, so take advantage of that.

Influence Presentations

The Influence type of personality also makes quick decisions. They'll want to know whom they are dealing with, so be sure to include a personal and company biography in the proposal package. Ask them what they want from the deal and mirror that back to them. Tell them you agree with their goals and compliment them on their choice of such a fine property. Stress factors like income stream and future appreciation of the property's value.

Compliance Presentations

This is apt to be your longest presentation. A Compliance person will have a formal demeanor and want to go through your proposal page by page. They may ask you about your methodology and expect you to have verified your sales and lease comparisons by using property tax records and the MLS. They may request an additional meeting to discuss the comparable properties.

To Compliance personalities, accuracy is next to godliness. They want all the facts fully documented and confirmed. They will want to look at your proposal, reread it, possibly make notes on it, and then and only then will they be in a position to make an informed business decision.

Steadiness Presentations

People who are heavily influenced by the Steadiness characteristics are going to want to hear all about how you as the practitioner put the proposal together. They will want to hear all the relevant facts about the market area and the details of the transaction.

Think of a tweed jacket wearing, pipe-smoking psychologist in a big overstuffed chair, and you'll have a good idea to whom you are presenting. As such, property owners who are high in the Steadiness traits want to know how your solution is going to help them. Don't count on them to make a rapid decision; they want to build a relationship with you and know that you genuinely care about them and their needs. These are people who care greatly about their family, so you might want to begin your presentation by asking questions about the various family members that you discussed during the first appointment. Spend the time to establish rapport before you begin your sales pitch.

> **CAUTION: Never tell the client that the opinion of value is based on your opinion. Always refer to the opinion of value as market derived. Remind the client that you don't make the market; you simply report the facts. Explain how the decision is purely arithmetic, practical and logical.**

IV. Ask for the Listing

Now that you've presented your proposal there's only one thing left to do; ask for the listing. For professionals who are new to the business, this is the hardest part of the meeting. Even if they've given a stellar presentation, fear of rejection holds them back. You have to get past this and move forward.

What is the worst that can happen? The seller says no. If that happens, forget about it and go on to the next deal. You have to understand that commercial real estate is a business that's driven by numbers. The number of proposals you do, the number of calls you make and the number of first appointments you make are the only determining factors in this business.

If you are to succeed in commercial investment real estate, you must strike out. You can't win every single listing presentation. It's physically impossible. Another thing to consider is that you may not want every assignment that you come across. Your only real commodity is your time, and you simply don't have enough time to satisfactorily service every client you encounter.

So, how do you ask for the listing? The first thing to do after the presentation is to remain silent. Let the client make the first comment. Let the client talk while you "actively" listen. The client will tell you precisely how to close them and ask for the listing. You may prompt them along; for example, if they were to say, "That seems to make sense," you may simply respond with "What should my next step be?" It can be as simple as that, while at other times it may require further dialogue. Listen to any objections and determine if they're real or smokescreens.

Commercial real estate is a series of give and take. You need to keep advancing toward your goal of obtaining the listing. Sometimes it may be lightning fast and other times it can drag on longer than you ever dreamed possible. Remember that Compliance and Steadiness personalities take longer to make decisions.

Step 7: Marketing the Listing

Most real estate sales associate's concept of marketing is placing a column-inch ad in the local newspaper, sitting back and waiting for the phone to ring. However, nothing could be further removed from the concept of marketing; it shouldn't be a passive activity. You need to make phone calls, design an ad that appeals to your target market and implement a long-term advertising campaign. Your campaign strategy should focus on selling the property, retaining the listing, promoting name recognition for yourself or your company and building brand awareness. Do you think the following ad accomplishes any of these things?

Multi-Family For Sale

26 Units all 2/2's

Great Investment

Bob's Realty & Investment

Phone: 555-555-5555

The only thing this ad conveys is that the listing sales associate is brand new or just doesn't care. If you want people to regard you as a seasoned professional, take some time to master this chapter.

You may have noticed that the property address isn't displayed in the ad; this is intentional. Many commercial properties have tenants, and you don't want them disturbed by people wandering around the building or apartment complex. Warehouses might be dangerous places for visitors. If you need to keep strangers away, leave the address out of the ad.

Once you have your campaign mapped out, calculate the budget needed to implement your plan. Present it to the sellers during the listing presentation and request that the sellers pay the expenses. Preferably, they will pay for the ads themselves as the payments come due so that you don't have to worry about reconciling an advance fee trust account or requesting reimbursement from the sellers. If they refuse to pay, at least you tried, and the next time you might be successful.

I. Phone Calls

The first thing you should do after you secure the listing is to access your database and call the owners of similar properties. If they own one investment property, they may want to own another, or they may know someone who's interested. You can also use your 1031 Exchange script in this situation if you discover during a phone call that someone wants to sell. In fact, if you want to focus on the tax benefits of a like-kind exchange, call all investors; not just the ones that already own a similar property. Call other sales associates who specialize in that type of property and let them know you have a new one entering the market. Make sure you have the property details and financial information in front of you when you call so that you can answer any questions quickly and accurately.

II. Design Considerations

The four psychological captivators that you should use during cold calls were discussed in Step 3. It is probably not a surprise to realize that these same four concepts also apply to advertising. In other words, your ad should grab an investor's attention (A), get him interested (I), encourage him to make a decision (D) and invite him to take action (A). Remember AIDA when you're drafting your ad and double check the copy when you're done to make sure you've covered all the bases.

Attention

People typically scan newspaper ads without paying much attention to the content until something about the ad catches their eye and makes them stop and read the details. That's why you always want to have a headline in your ad, and you want it to be bold, shocking or informative; something that will make them stop and read the ad. Add color to the ad, and it will stand out against the sea of gray newspaper print. Instead of using tired expressions like "Owner says sell" or "Reduced for quick sale," put a unique spin on the property with a statement like "It ain't pretty, but it sure makes money" or "Ugly building needs attention." Use attention-getting words; new, free, unique, profit, easy and one-of-a-kind are all good examples that you can use.

Interest

Once you have the buyers' attention, you need to pique their interest. Remember, your target audience is investors, and they want to know what's in it for them if they buy your property. Talk about making or saving money, low building expenses, below-market rents or 100 percent leased. Your ultimate goal is to get them to call you for more information.

Decision

What can you offer them that will make them pick up the phone and call you? There are a number of things: free income analysis (which you have already completed for the listing proposal), free market analysis (which you have also already completed for the listing presentation), free property inspection or free appraisal. The last two will cost you money out of your pocket, but they usually aren't completed until the buyer has already signed a contract and applied for a loan.

Action

At the bottom of the ad, you want to issue a personal invitation to the prospect to reach out to you. Consequently, you can phrase the last line as "Call me, John Doe, at 555-555-5555." You're not ordering them to call; you are asking them. You are making a connection with them.

Now take a look at the revised ad. Do you think it will get more responses than the previous one?

Investor's Dream

Multi-Family

Rent Below Market

20% Upside Potential

Bob's Realty & Investment

Call Me, Bob Smith, at 555-555-5555.

III. Property Description

Unless you have a large budget, your newspaper ads are most likely limited to just a few words, which includes the company name, your name and phone number. That doesn't leave you much space to talk about the property. You have more leeway, however, in other types of advertising; MLS listings, postcards, flyers, letters and emails provide sufficient room for a more extensive description of the property.

Most investors care more about the benefits and advantages of owning a property than they care about the property's features. The color of a building isn't as important as the generated cash flow. If you are going to describe a property's features, then you need to carry through and mention the benefits of advantages of ownership. Consider the following example.

Suppose that you have just received a listing for a building with the following features: two-story, C-class commercial office building, solid concrete block construction, 113,000 sq. ft., located on a corner lot of a busy street, city water and sewer, central air, 40 parking spaces, phone, Internet and cable wiring, 220 electric, commercial-grade carpeting, marble lobby, tile bathrooms and 120 foot frontage on the street. Given these facts, what do you want to stress in the property description? Do you emphasize the fact that it's on a busy street, or the benefit that the increased visibility gives you the advantage that the property is easy to find and saves clients time. Take a moment to look at the following table and see if you can come up with additional features, benefits and advantages.

	FEATURE	BENEFIT	ADVANTAGE
1	located on corner intersection	high visibility	easy to find, saves clients time
2	concrete block construction	fire, wind and termite resistant	low insurance and maintenance costs
3	high density traffic count	high visibility and exposure	attractive to tenants
4	over 40 parking spaces	plenty of room for customers	attractive to tenants
5	marble lobby, central air, carpeting	attractive to tenants	easier to lease, lower vacancy rates, increased cash flow

IV. Sources

To market your listing effectively, you need to make sure that you reach potential investors, real estate brokers and sales associates. You can do this in a number of different ways including the Internet, newspapers, snail mail and signs. Make sure you display the property on your own website and blog. If you don't have a blog, start one. There are a number of different blogging options, but Google provides unlimited, easy-to-use, high-visibility blogging capability when you sign up for a free account.

MLS

The Multiple Listing Service (MLS) is the first place that many Realtors go to when they are searching for properties. Some local Realtor associations may even have transparent, free tools that syndicate the listing to other sites including Trulia, Zillow, Yahoo and the New York Times. Check with your association and see if this benefit is included in your membership fee. Upload multiple photographs of the property and remember to stress the benefits and advantages of owning the property. Ensure that your contact information is correct. In order to list in the MLS, you must display the selling agent's commission and agree to cooperate with them. If you want to maintain control of the transaction, don't grant permission in the MLS for other professionals to advertise your listing.

Websites

The Internet is a marvelous marketing tool that has revolutionized the industry. Many of the sites, however, may allow a visitor to browse listings for free, but require that you pay a membership fee in order to post a listing.

- www.realup.com
- www.loopnet.com
- www.activerain.com
- www.cityfeet.com
- www.costar.com
- www.cimls.com
- www.catylist.com
- www.craigslist.com
- www.postlets.com
- www.buildingsearch.com
- www.propertyline.com
- www.iciworld.com
- www.allrealestateonline.com

Newspapers

For many properties, small classified ads may be as effective as the more expensive half-page spreads. Rates may differ depending on which day of the week the ad runs, so call the advertising department and ask for a rate sheet that includes size, color and day. Remember to include an attention-getting headline. If you are going to test the response to different ads, code them so you can track responses. When an interested party calls for more information, ask him what number appears in the bottom right-hand corner of the ad. That's where you want to place an alphanumeric code that will enable you to collect the response rate to an individual ad. If you've ever ordered anything from a catalog, you were asked for this type of number. This is done for marketing purposes when the company mails different versions of a catalog.

Postcards

Postcards are an effective marketing tool that you can mail to a specific type of customer; target individuals who are already investors. You can create an initial mailing list from the address on the deed, which is usually a matter of public record. Search the property tax records for commercial property near your listing, record the owner's name and address, and add the information to your database or spreadsheet. There are many online mailing services where you can create a postcard from scratch or use one of the existing templates; ExpressCopy is one vendor's site that produces beautiful full-color laminated postcards. The user uploads a file of mailing addresses and schedules the mailing date. Jobs can be scheduled far in advance, so you don't have to remember to send them out multiple times, if that is your intent. If the property sells, you can cancel the scheduled printing.

> Website: http://expresscopy.com/

Letters

Letters are an excellent way to build brand recognition and let prospective customers know who you are and what you have to offer in addition to the listing that you're promoting. Make sure that you use letterhead stationery and spellcheck the content. The letter can be anywhere from one page to more than ten pages. However, if you bore them, that may cause your letter to be filed in the trashcan.

Email

Email is another tool in your marketing arsenal. The good news is that it's free; the bad news is that you may get fined or blacklisted. At the very least, your email may be caught in spam filters and never read. In addition, Internet Service Providers (ISP) like Comcast, Google or Hotmail, may limit the number of emails that you are allowed to send in a day. Ideally, you would like to collect metrics regarding the number of times your email was opened or forwarded. Links that connect the email to your professional social media sites and websites are also useful additions. You can implement these ideas yourself, or you can use an Email Service Provider (ESP) that provides the mechanisms for monitoring email reads and provides connectivity buttons to link the reader with your social media sites. Whether you choose to do everything yourself or use an Email Service Provider, you need to be aware of some basic laws and best practices.

- CAN-SPAM Act

    The CAN-SPAM Act is a federal law that passed in 2003 and regulates commercial email format, establishes consumer's rights and sets penalties and fines for violators. Protect yourself and read the law before you start an email campaign. In essence, the sender's name and company mailing address must be included in the email; the subject line must give an accurate depiction of the contents of the email, and recipients must have a way of opting-out of receiving any more emails from that sender. The sender must honor their request to be removed from the mailing list within 10 business days, and their email address can't be sold or added to any other list.

- Blacklisting

    Blacklisting is the practice of blocking email from reaching the intended recipient. An individual may be able to block unwanted emails, and a company can set up a block so that it doesn't reach anyone using the company's email server. Blocking also happens when your ISP thinks you are sending spam messages and blocks all of your outgoing emails; you're not informed and have no idea that your emails aren't being received. This happens when you exceed the allowable number of emails in a day; this number varies among ISPs. That means that none of your gmail, hotmail or comcast emails are reaching your prospective buyers, and you don't know it. Check with your provider or search the Internet for ways to detect if you are currently blacklisted and for the proper way to get the emails flowing once again.

- Spam Filters

    Spam is unwanted or unsolicited emails, and various types of filters "capture" suspected spam and re-route it to a separate file in your email software. Many people never bother to look in this spam file, so any tagged emails are never seen. Your goal is to minimize the possibility of your emails being considered spam. You can most easily do this by using a tool provided by an ESP that searches for the presence of certain words that may be flagged by one of the filters.

- Email Service Providers

Email Service Providers (ESP) take a lot of the guess work out of an email campaign. One major benefit is that you can send an unlimited number of emails at a time using an online ESP application; you're not limited by an ISP's daily allowable limit. Your ESP should be able to monitor which emails are opened, check emails for spam trigger words and allow you to easily place social media buttons on the email that enable the reader to broadcast your information to a wider audience. Two well-regarded vendors are Constant Contact and MailChimp. Constant Contact has a 60-day free trial but charges a monthly fee based on volume once the trial period expires. MailChimp is a powerful, free service.

> Website: http://www.constantcontact.com
> Website: http://mailchimp.com/

Social Media

Post your listing on your social media sites (Facebook, LinkedIn, Twitter, blog). Your email audience will probably be investors. If one of them "Likes" your email or posted listing, it will appear on his Facebook page and might be seen by other investors. If one of those investors "Likes" it, the content will appear on his own page, and before you know it, your listing is spread far and wide over the Internet.

Signs

For Sale signs are an easy way to market your listing. Position them so that they receive the maximum exposure and make sure that the contact information is correct. If your brokerage firm and state real estate law allow, have your cell phone number on the sign without the company's number. That way, you won't miss any leads. Banners hanging down from the top of the property can also be used to good effect.

Brochures

You'll need to prepare information to give prospective buyers and other Realtors. This can be a subset of your listing presentation; just include photographs and features, and omit the pricing, comparables and marketing sections. Loopnet creates nice brochures and flyers for premium members, or you can print flyers from your MLS.

V. Frequency

Marketing experts agree that it usually takes multiple exposures to the same message before a consumer acts. Therefore, you need to get your name and property in front of them a number of times. In other words, you need to design a marketing campaign and stick to it.

VI. Plan

Include the marketing plan as part of your listing presentation and give a detailed account of what you intend to do. If the sellers are talking to other brokers and comparing listing presentations, you want your marketing section to win the day. Ask your broker if she has a template, before you reinvent the wheel. Otherwise, feel free to revise the following plan to meet your needs. This section will detail a six-week plan, but you may want to present a six-month plan in your listing presentation. CityFeet specifies the more than 200 sites where it syndicates your listing. It might be a good idea to list all these websites as the final page of the plan; it's a very impressive list and is something that your competitors might not include in their presentation.

Week One

Your sales associate will install a For Sale sign on the property and post the property listing in the Multiple Listing Service (MLS), our corporate website and 13 additional sites that include CityFeet.com and LoopNet.com. In turn, CityFeet syndicates the listing to more than 200 additional locations including regional newspapers. Your sales associate has a premium membership in LoopNet, which is a listing website that receives more than 2 million visitors a month. Members can post listings and receive the contact information for registered buyers and brokers who have searched for listings similar to yours. These contacts will become part of an on-going email campaign.

The most likely buyer of your property is another investor. Therefore, your sales associate will spend a considerable amount of time over the next four weeks searching the property tax records and developing a database of prospects who own properties similar to yours. This contact list will be the basis of the subsequent letter, postcard and phone call campaigns. Your sales associate will develop a presentation package for prospects who are viewing the property.

You will receive the first of the weekly emails that describes the efforts your agent has made on your behalf during the week. The update will include the names of prospects and brokers who have contacted your agent regarding the property. The weekly report will also include information on the number of people who viewed the property in the MLS.

Week Two

Your sales associate will continue to develop a database of existing investors and develop a postcard to use in the mailing campaign. You will be sent a copy of the postcard as well as any other material that is developed for distribution. LoopNet contacts will be emailed property information. This will become a weekly event as new prospects visit the Loopnet website each week. Flyers will be emailed to other commercial real estate sales people in the area. You will be sent your weekly update.

Week Three

Postcards will be sent to the database of investors who own property similar to yours. Your sales associate will continue to monitor LoopNet visitors and email new prospects. All phone calls and emails will be answered in a timely fashion, and your weekly update will contain the names of any contacts. Your sales associate will attend the monthly commercial Realtor networking breakfast and distribute brochures to interested parties.

Week Four

Your property listing will continue to be maintained on Internet websites, and LoopNet visitors will be emailed the property information. Your sales associate will develop a newspaper ad and monitor the responses to the postcard mailings. You will receive your weekly update.

Week Five

Your real estate associate will develop a letter to be mailed to potential investors. The newspaper ad will be placed (if appropriate), and Loopnet marketing will continue. You will receive a weekly update email.

Week Six

- Maintain Internet listings.

- Send Loopnet emails to new registered visitors.

- Mail letter to existing investors.

- Email weekly status report.

Step 8: Presenting the Offer

State laws may prohibit sales associates and brokers from drafting contracts, but you are permitted to fill in the blanks on the documents for your buyers and present offers to your sellers. You are not allowed to give a legal opinion and must be careful to avoid the temptation. If your client is using an attorney for the closing, email all the documents to his lawyer for review. Don't depend on your client forwarding materials to him.

I. Letter of Intent

The letter of intent (LOI) is an optional form that's not used in residential real estate but frequently makes an appearance in commercial transactions. You can think of it as a precursor to a formal offer. The basic terms are stated in plain English and then discussed. If the parties reach an agreement, the buyer submits an offer that incorporates the agreed-upon items. Real estate brokers can write LOIs if state law allows, and your local Realtor association may have a short form you can download. Complicated transactions may have an LOI that is 10 pages or more, but 1-2 pages are more commonly used.

Terms

Basic information in the LOI includes the following items.

- Buyer Name
- Seller Name
- Property Address
- Legal Description
- Lists of Included and Excluded Personal Property
- Purchase Price
- Earnest Money Deposit(s)
- Financing

- Closing Date

- Broker Commission and the Party Responsible for Paying It

- Any Special Clauses

- Attachments

- Buyer Signature and Date

- Seller Signature and Date

Disclaimer

You need to make sure the letter states that this is a non-binding agreement and not a legal contract. Include language that makes it clear the letter has no further effect if all parties don't sign a formal contract within 30 days. However, be aware that based on the behavior and intent of the parties some judges have ruled that some LOIs were binding even with a disclaimer. Consult an attorney if you have any doubts.

II. Sale and Purchase Contract

Most residential real estate contracts are ones approved by the state's Realtor association. However, custom contracts are often used for commercial real estate transactions. While you may start out using a Realtor commercial contract, eventually you may find issues a standard contract doesn't address to your satisfaction. As you gain more experience and are exposed to different types of situations, you'll probably want to speak with an attorney about drafting a contract that reflects your preferences. **Don't do this without your broker's permission.**

The offer is written on a sale and purchase contract that becomes binding when all parties agree to the terms and sign on the dotted line. However, there may be an unexpected twist in your commercial deal. Don't be surprised if you're representing a buyer, and the listing broker requires you to use his contract. That's perfectly legal and is simply an indication that the broker wants to control the situation. In this case, you can be sure the contract favors the seller. Have the buyer's attorney review it and make any suggested changes before your buyer signs the offer. Just because it's the seller's contract doesn't mean the wording can't be modified.

There are usually many different sections in a commercial contract. The next few pages highlight some common areas of concern and discuss any differences between commercial and residential practices as it applies to those items.

Parties and Property

This section is critically important, and you must ensure that there are no typos. Whenever possible, copy and paste information from the property tax record into the contract.

- Seller

    Commercial sellers are usually corporations, and the authorized officers of the corporation sign the contract. Be sure to include any corporate name suffixes including Inc., Corp., LLP. or LLC.

- Buyer

    Unlike the seller, the buyer may make an offer prior to forming a corporation. Consequently, if you're representing the buyer, make sure that the contract is assignable. This means that the contractual rights can be transferred to another party who will be bound by the existing terms. You might want to submit the offer as: John Buyer on behalf of an entity to be formed.

- Folio

    The folio number or assessor's parcel number is on the property tax record.

- Legal Description

    A street address does not adequately describe a property. The legal description must also be included and should be copied from the tax record. If you are using a preprinted form that doesn't have enough space to type a lengthy description, include an addendum or insert the full legal description in a comments area.

- Personal Property

    If the buyer wishes the offer to include any of the seller's personal property, you should list those items. It's often difficult to determine what is a fixture that should be conveyed with the building, and what is personal property. If the buyer really wants something, list it on the offer in order to avoid any confusion at a later date.

Purchase Terms

This is the part of the contract that garners the most attention from the sellers and buyers. It's straightforward enough for everyone to understand, which is not necessarily the case with other sections.

- Price

    The purchase price includes all the money that the buyer intends to bring to the table including mortgage loans. If the real estate market is slow with an abundance of inventory, or if the property has been listed for a long time, this offer price is likely to be less than the list price.

- Escrow

    Escrow money is known by many names including earnest money deposit, good faith money or cash down payment. These funds come from the buyer and are held in a trust account that is maintained by a real estate broker, title company or attorney. The buyers forfeit this money if they withdraw from the contract without a legitimate reason. If the transaction closes, this money is applied towards the buyer's closing costs. The name of the escrow agent should be on the contract.

    Try to have the buyers contribute as much as possible to the escrow account; the more skin they have in the game the less likely they are to walk away from the deal. Second deposits are common in commercial real estate and are frequently timed to come due once the inspection period ends.

    Commercial transactions have a concept known as "**hard escrow**" or "**pass through deposits**" in which the escrow money "passes through" to the seller and becomes nonrefundable after a certain event or period of time (inspection period, property appraisal or environmental survey.) If you are representing the seller and if the practice is legal in your state, you might want to try to negotiate these terms since it gives the buyer a tremendous incentive to close the deal.

- Financing

    The first page of the contract typically includes a section that summarizes all the financing that the buyer hopes to attain. This can include new financing from a lender, an assumption of the seller's loan or seller's financing. The details of the anticipated loans are described in a separate financing contingency section.

- Cash to Close

    Cash to close is the amount of money the buyer needs at closing without considering any prorations. It's calculated by subtracting the escrow and financing amounts from the purchase price.

Time for Acceptance

The time for acceptance should be kept reasonably short so that the seller doesn't have time to use the buyer's offer as an opportunity to instigate a bidding war. On the other hand, commercial contracts are frequently not familiar preprinted forms, and you need to allow the seller's attorney enough time to review it; five days should be ample time for the seller to reply.

Closing Date

Long closing dates favor the buyer, and shorter durations favor the seller. If you're representing the buyer, you want ample time for loan approval and inspections. The seller is at risk during a long delay; there's always a chance that the property will be damaged or that a zoning change devalues the property. Either one of these circumstances is normally considered a legitimate reason for the buyer to cancel the contract and have the earnest money refunded. Most commercial deals can usually close within 75 days of the effective date, which is the date the signed contract has been delivered to both the buyer and seller. However, this timeframe doesn't apply to large tracts of undeveloped land that may take more than a year or two to close.

Many contracts state that **"time is of the essence."** Failure of one of the parties to perform within the specified time period may be grounds for breach of contract if the materially damaged party files a lawsuit. In addition to the closing date, there are usually many other deadlines in a contract including the number of days for loan approval, title commitment, appraisal, survey and inspections. Speak to an attorney if you don't understand the possible consequences of missing a date in a "time is of the essence" contract.

Financing Contingencies

Commercial loans for the purchase of income-producing properties have significantly different underwriting requirements than residential mortgage loans. Approval may be difficult to obtain so you need to make sure that the contract contains a financing contingency that allows the buyer's earnest money to be returned to them if they fail to obtain a loan after making a good faith effort to do so. You can make the process a little smoother by having a lender pre-qualify a buyer for a loan.

- Qualification

    One of the easiest criteria to check is the experience level of the buyer, which is not an issue that ever comes up during the purchase of a home. However, commercial lending is different from residential. For example, if you have an investor who wants to purchase a 20-unit apartment building, and they have no prior landlord or property management experience, the loan may be denied. You might show them 3-plex or 4-plex multifamily housing instead and let them improve their resume before trying to purchase a larger building. These smaller properties are approved according to residential underwriting criteria, which is not concerned with a buyer's prior investment experience.

    Projected cash flow is another concern with commercial investment properties. In particular, the lenders want the building to generate positive cash flow after paying for building expenses and mortgage payments. This benchmark is known as the debt service coverage ratio and is calculated as NOI/annual debt service. A number less than 1.0 indicates negative cash flow and is likely to result in a denial of the loan application. The preferred ratio is 1.15 or higher.

    The buyers should be prepared to submit the prior 3-5 years of personal and corporate income tax returns (if they exist). The lender will also check the buyers' credit reports. In a tight lending market, the applicant may need a personal net worth approximately equal to the value of the property.

- New Loan

    Commercial funding may come from a variety of sources including the seller, commercial banks, independent lenders, insurance companies and investment consortiums. A commercial broker can work with your buyer to determine the most appropriate source of funds. Most buyers will need a minimum 25 percent down payment for a new commercial loan. Make sure that your buyer is aware of this cash requirement before you start showing properties in their stated price range.

- Loan Assumption

    The seller's mortgage loan may be assumable by a qualified buyer. There are three possible types of assumptions. The first method is simply called an assumption, and both the buyer and seller assume liability for the note. The second occurs when the seller is released from liability, and this is known as assumption with novation. The third approach is rare and is called taking property "subject to" existing financing. In this case, no one is personally liable for the note; the buyer agrees to make the mortgage payments, but the lender can't sue them for any part of the unpaid balance if they default. However, the lender probably can foreclose on the property and evict the occupants.

- Specificity

If you are representing the buyer, you want the financing terms to be as specific as possible. State the maximum interest rate, term and type of loan that your buyer needs; if they fail to obtain an approval that matches those specifications, they can most likely cancel the contract without penalty. At the same time, they retain the choice to proceed with the deal and accept alternate loan terms.

On the other hand, if you are one of the listing brokers that insist your contract is used, you want the financing terms to be as vague as possible, so that the buyer has less "wiggle" room. In this case, the contract might state that the buyer may cancel if they don't receive approval for a loan at prevailing interest rates. That's a lot less specific than stating that cancellation is possible if a buyer doesn't receive a 5 percent interest rate, 30 year fixed rate loan. Specific terms favor the buyer while vague specifications favor the seller.

- Limitations

In some cases, the buyer needs to obtain construction financing in addition to the purchase price. For example, a doctor makes an offer to buy a restaurant with the intent to convert it into a medical office. The cost to gut the interior and renovate it to suit his purpose may actually exceed the purchase price. However, the offer price and financing contingency reflect the amount needed to purchase the property without including the build-out costs. If the property value is $300,000, that may be an appropriate offer price; the total $600,000 loan amount doesn't appear on a typical contract. If he can only obtain a $300,000 loan, then he's the proud owner of a restaurant. He probably can't cancel the contract because he couldn't obtain the additional remodeling money. Most sellers won't allow the additional funding to be a contingency. Make sure the attorney reviews the contract and explains the situation to your buyer.

- Loan Approval Date

Approval for a commercial mortgage loan may take longer than a residential loan. If your buyer has already been pre-approved for a loan, the required time may be reduced by two weeks. Allow at least 30 days for loan approval. If the loan has not been approved within this window, either party may be able to cancel the contract.

Inspection Contingencies

This section of the contract is the portion of an offer that differs the most radically from residential purchase contracts. Federal commercial real estate law doesn't require sellers to disclose existing problems, so buyers need more protections in the contract and must assume the responsibility for uncovering any damage or hazards. This includes discovering any environmental damage caused by hazardous substances contaminating the land surrounding the structure. In particular, buyers who purchase properties that were once the site for a gas station, dry cleaner or manufacturing plant need to be particularly cautious. These environmental concerns are discussed in more detail in the next chapter.

Short inspection periods favor the seller while longer timeframes are better for the buyer. If the property is occupied by tenants, the time for document inspection will take longer than if the property is vacant because individual leases need to be verified.

- Property Inspection

  There are three basic types of property inspection contingencies. The first type is a strict as-is contract in which the buyer waives the right to inspect the property and accepts the property as it is. The second type is an as-is contract with the right to conduct inspections within a specified time period; the buyer can cancel the contract if the inspections uncover unacceptable problems with the property, and the seller is not obligated to contribute any money toward repairs. The third approach allows inspections and requires the seller to contribute a specified amount toward repairs; this is not used as often in commercial transactions as the as-is type of contract.

  In general, an inspector should look at the plumbing and electrical systems, elevators, roof and foundation. A different inspector may be required to perform the environmental survey, and the lender may insist that the buyer use the services of a particular company.

- Document Inspection

  Unless an investor is purchasing space for his sole use, the property's generated cash flow is usually a major factor in the buyer's decision-making process. Consequently, the buyer needs to verify that the current net operating income meets his investment goals. Therefore, the contract needs to allow adequate time for the buyer and his representatives to examine the books and records related to the building's expenses and income.

Whenever there are tenants, the seller needs to produce the rent roll including an accounting of the security deposits and other collected fees. In addition, the seller should hand over any existing documentation on the tenants such as credit reports and financial statements. Leases should be verified by the tenants who certify that the information provided to the prospective buyer is accurate. This may appear in the contract as a separate estoppel certificate contingency that is binding on the seller and requires the seller to obtain tenant verification. This task can, however, be assumed by the unbiased purchaser.

Many residential real estate sales associates and brokers are familiar with condominium sales. However, they may be surprised that a condominium association governs some commercial retail properties. The buyer has the right to review the condominium documents and be informed of maintenance fees.

- Federal, State and Local Laws

The buyer needs to verify that there are no fines or building code violations on the property. Some violations take a considerable amount of time to correct, and the buyer inherits the problem if it's not resolved before closing. If the violations are severe, it's possible that the property has already been condemned by the city.

Commercial real estate professionals are more concerned with zoning issues than their residential counterparts. The buyer's representative should contact the city's zoning and planning department and obtain written verification of the current zoning and approved uses for the property site. If the anticipated use isn't approved for the site, the buyer's attorney needs to request a change from the city. This is likely to extend the time needed for closing, since the buyer will want the change approved before the sale is finalized. Contact city services for an estimate of the approval time. Be particularly alert if the buyer plans to implement a manufacturing facility within a business district. Zoning is also an issue for restaurants and medical offices since they require more parking spaces than retail shops and general office buildings. Keep this in mind when you are initially looking for properties.

The Americans with Disabilities Act (ADA) is another issue that affects commercial practitioners more than residential professionals. This is a comprehensive piece of civil rights legislation that covers many areas of discrimination from employment, public transportation, access to public buildings and wheelchair-accessible bathrooms. It's the last two items that will have an impact on a buyer's purchase of a commercial building.

New construction and alterations must adhere to the ADA design guides, which include entrance ramps and bathroom stalls that are large enough to maneuver a wheelchair. Buildings built before 1992 that serve the public are required to implement accessibility changes if the cost is readily achievable. Your buyer's general contractor should be aware of the rules if alterations are planned; however, it's worth mentioning the law to your client who can then discuss it further with a real estate attorney. The penalties for failing to conform to ADA regulations can be quite expensive.

- Due Diligence Period

  The due diligence period is also known as the feasibility period and refers to the time during which the buyer can inspect the property, examine documents and investigate the existence of any zoning or code violation issues. A contract that favors the seller may have different specified deadlines for each type of inspection contingency. Alternatively, buyers' contracts may have just one overall deadline (the due diligence period) in which to complete all the required inspections. Whichever party you represent, make sure you pay attention to the deadlines.

FIRPTA

The Foreign Investment in Real Property Tax Act of 1980 (FIRPTA) is an IRS regulation that mandates the collection of a capital gains tax from sellers of real property at the time of closing. The law requires that the buyer withhold 10 percent of the purchase price on most foreign-owned property. If the seller believes this amount to be excessive, they can apply to the IRS for a withholding certificate that approves a lower amount of withholding. If you represent foreign owners, be sure that you inform them of the FIRPTA rules and include the information when you list the property in order to avoid confusion at the closing. The title company or buyer's attorney usually handles transferring the payment to the IRS, but the buyer may be held accountable if payment is not made.

There are legal ways in which foreigners can shelter the property from capital gains tax, and you should have them consult with a knowledgeable attorney before purchasing. Sellers may also engage in a "1031 like-kind exchange" that allows for the deferral of capital gains payments, but they need to plan for this prior to the closing.

Radon

Radon is a carcinogenic gas that's released into the air during the breakdown of radioactive uranium, which is a naturally occurring element found in the soil of all 50 states. The U.S. Surgeon General states that it is the second largest cause of lung cancer, which may arise from the radioactive particles irritating lung tissue and setting the stage for the development of cancer.

Gas enters the building through cracks in the foundation and walls or through openings around pipes. The buyer must be allowed sufficient time to test for the presence of the gas, but the seller has no obligation to pay for the test or to remedy the situation if high levels are detected. However, the presence of radon may open the door to negotiating a price reduction.

III. Negotiations

Negotiating skills are learned over time, and there's no blueprint to follow. Every deal is different and dependent on a number of factors. The motivation of the seller and buyer are hugely important; how badly they want to sell or buy a particular property plays a major role during the negotiation process, and it's your job to try to determine the opposing side's level of motivation. Local market conditions also exert a considerable influence on the process; you need to know the current inventory of listed properties and the average days on market and sale price for recently closed transactions. Financing plays a role as well; a cash deal is more favorable to the seller and will generally close at a lower sale price because there is no financing contingency that provides the buyer with a potential opportunity to cancel the contract. While there are a number of influences affecting negotiations, everything starts with the list price.

List Price

When a seller's representative presents a listing proposal, it includes a suggested listed price that is partially based on current market conditions and the calculated net operating income that's generated by the building and its tenants. The vacancy rate and quality of the tenants play a major role in the value of the property; a fully leased building is usually more attractive to an investor than a half-empty one. A strongly motivated seller may decide to list it for a lesser amount in an attempt to sell the property more quickly. On the other hand, a less motivated owner may list it significantly higher in order to test the waters; this is usually not a good situation for either the seller's or the buyer's representative. The seller may not be willing to lower the price until it has been on the market for a considerable amount of time. At that point, the buyers may have the impression that there is something wrong with the property or that the seller must be getting anxious; consequently, the offer price will be lower than it would have been if the property was reasonably priced in the first place.

Offer

When the buyer is to be the sole tenant of the property, the offer price is likely to be based primarily on the recent sales price of comparable properties. However, if the property is leased, the buyer may base the offer on his desired rate of return. In Step 5 of this text, we discussed the cap rate and IRV formula. Therefore, if you recall those calculations and the listing agent states that the NOI is $30,000 a year and your investor wants a 7 percent capitalization rate of return on his investment, a reasonable offer price is likely to be $30,000/.07 or $429,000. This is the most basic type of calculation and doesn't take future appreciation and resale value into account, but if you're just starting to work in commercial real estate and aren't yet familiar with more advanced analysis, it will have to do.

If you're representing the buyer, you need to see how that calculated value compares with actual recent sales and the seller's list price; you certainly don't want to offer more than list price. Make an effort to discover the history of the property; if the seller has been dropping the price, it's an indication that he's motivated to sell so consider a low offer. Properties that have been recently listed or not subjected to price drops, may not warrant a low-ball offer that could antagonize the seller. Take your cues from the listing agent; he may give you an indication of the seller's eagerness to close. This initial offer should be in writing, signed and dated by the buyers after an attorney review.

Counteroffer

People like to negotiate, and many buyers feel disappointed if the seller accepts their first offer; they assume that the offer was too high if it's immediately accepted. That's not true, but it is the perception. Unless you have already negotiated a letter of intent, the seller is apt to counter the buyer's offer. In commercial real estate contracts, timeframes and escrow amounts are frequently negotiated in addition to the price.

A common pricing counteroffer is to "split the difference." Suppose a property is listed for $500,000, and the initial offer is $450,000. More often than not, the seller will come back with a value of $475,000. The buyer was $50,000 below list, so the seller halved that amount. Similarly, the buyer's counter to the seller's $475,000 is most likely to be $462, 500. There was a $25,000 difference between the offers, so the buyers halved that amount and added it to their initial offer of $450,000. Keep this common pattern of behavior in mind when you start negotiations, and you can more accurately predict the final accepted price.

When the sellers and the buyers agree on the terms, the sellers sign and date the offer and the buyer and seller initial any changes incorporated into the contract. Once this is completed, you have in your hands a legally binding commercial contract. Congratulations! Now you have to get it closed.

Step 9: Closing the Transaction

Don't go spending your commission money just because you have a signed agreement. There are many pitfalls that you may encounter over the next few weeks that might cause the deal to crash and burn. Every deal is different and new problems pop up when you least expect them, but that is part of the reason why the real estate business is a fun and challenging career. You never know what to expect. With experience, you will recognize the warning signs that there is danger ahead, and you can perhaps avoid hitting the bumps in the road that can throw you off course.

One of the best ways to prepare yourself is to study this chapter, which presents some potential obstacles and procedures that you may not encounter in residential real estate transactions. If you have questions, talk to your broker, colleagues and real estate attorneys. Search out commercial real estate organizations and journals. Network, take classes and read books; soak up information from every reputable source you can find. Stick with it, and you'll eventually master the process. It's like any other skill; all it takes is dedication and practice.

I.   Tenants

If there are tenants in the building, the due diligence period needs to be longer than it would be for a vacant building. Leases need to be verified, square footage of the leased space documented, and data collected on individual security deposits and advance rents that have already been paid to the landlord. In some cases, the seller may request that each tenant signs an estoppel certificate asserting that the lease-related information in the estoppel letter is true. In other cases where this process may confuse short-term tenants, the buyer may choose to accept a seller's affidavit that the provided lease information is accurate. If there is any doubt, the buyer and real estate sales associate can provide their own forms for the tenants to sign, or they can call the tenants to verify the seller-provided information.

II.   Environmental Issues

There may be many hidden toxins associated with a property, and you want to encourage your buyer to test for these substances during the due diligence period. No owner wants to be responsible for tenants' illnesses, and the cost to remedy the situation may be prohibitively expensive. The best course of action is for the seller to hire qualified inspectors who will examine the building and grounds while there is still time to terminate the contract or to negotiate a reduction in sales price in order to pay for the cleanup.

Radon

Radon is a naturally occurring carcinogenic radioactive gas that's released from the soil as uranium decays. It enters buildings through cracks in the foundation and walls, openings around joints and wall cavities. The Surgeon General states that radon is the second leading cause of lung cancer in the United States; not as bad as cigarette smoking but more lethal than exposure to second hand smoke. Radon is found throughout the United States.

Buyers can purchase inexpensive radon test kits at many home repair and hardware stores. Follow the directions on the box and position the monitor in an appropriate place. Alternatively, your state radon office may have a list of approved testers who can monitor the air within the property.

Remedial measures can be expensive and should be performed by a qualified radon mitigation expert. Possible solutions involve sealing cracks and installing venting systems.

Asbestos

Asbestos is another carcinogenic substance that can cause lung cancer and other diseases. Because of its strength and fire resistance, this mineral fiber is used in a variety of applications including wall insulation, vinyl tiles, roofing and siding shingles, and textured wall and ceiling paint. Problems arise when the material is disturbed, and the fibers are released into the air where occupants can inhale them. This is of particular concern if the buyer plans to demolish, repair or remodel the property.

The Clean Air Act requires the U.S. Environmental Protection Agency (EPA) to regulate the release of toxic air pollutants including asbestos. Consequently, contractors must test for the presence of asbestos in commercial properties that are to be torn down or renovated. If the levels and location of the substance exceed accepted guidelines, the material must be removed and disposed of in a federally-approved manner. Be aware that this can significantly increase the estimated construction costs and may provide the buyer with an opportunity to negotiate a reduction in the property's sales price.

Mold

Mold spores thrive in warm humid environments, and active growth is likely to occur near plumbing leaks, shower stalls, open windows and roof leaks. The federal government doesn't set acceptable levels of mold, but mild cases should be cleaned with water and detergent since mold spores can cause allergic reactions and respiratory problems including asthma. Moldy carpets should be replaced. Contact a professional mold mitigation expert for additional advice.

Environmental Site Assessments

While radon, asbestos and mold are issues that frequently need to be addressed in both residential and commercial real estate transactions, water and land pollution problems are more apt to occur at commercial and industrial sites. A series of environmental site assessments search for possible contamination and monitors the cleanup process if any toxicity is uncovered. As a general rule, a Phase I environmental site assessment should be conducted during the due diligence period for all commercial and industrial transactions even if it's not requested by the lender.

This is a highly recommended practice because of federal liability laws. The Comprehensive Environmental Response, Compensation, and Liability Act (CERCLA) along with the Superfund Amendments and Reauthorization Act of 1986 may provide that the current owners of a property are responsible for all payments related to removing the pollution even if they didn't cause it. In some cases, the cost of the remedial actions may exceed the price of the building.

- Phase I

    A Phase I Environmental Site Assessment consists of four basic steps. The specialist first searches the records for the past uses of the property and determines whether that investigation raises any red flags. Neighboring property records are also researched since the possibility exists that contamination on one lot may spread to adjacent land. Aerial photographs are collected to document the historical development of the property, and the investigator searches public records for any recorded health or safety information related to the property.

    The inspector visits the property to search for any visible signs of contamination. The inside of the structure is ignored, which is why separate asbestos, radon and mold inspections may be ordered. Instead, the assessor walks the property and takes photographs to document the condition of the land. No soil or water testing occurs during Phase I.

    At this point, tenants and property managers are interviewed and any concerns documented. Additional calls may be made to various city departments including health, fire and water, and past or outstanding issues are noted.

    Finally, the inspector prepares and submits the report that includes a discussion of possible issues and recommended follow-up actions.

- Phase II

    If the Phase I investigation uncovers possible pollution problems, a Phase II site assessment is ordered to determine the level of potential risk to the environment. Soil and water are tested for the presence of pollutants. In some cases, a potential buyer may order a Phase II to document any background contamination and establish a baseline level even if a Phase I raised no issues.

- Phase III

    Phase III further documents the extent of the contamination and notifies the appropriate local, state and federal regulatory agencies. A removal plan is devised, approved and implemented, and the government agencies are notified when the process is complete.

III. Documents

If you are selling an investment property, do yourself a favor and make the process smoother by getting the due diligence material together during the marketing of the property. That way when an offer is made and accepted you can deliver the due diligence material when the contract is fully executed. If you do that, the buyers have no excuse that they didn't get the materials they need and consequently, need an extension of the due diligence period. In Chapter 4, we recommended that you email the seller a first appointment checklist requesting him to have a number of documents ready for you to copy if the meeting seemed likely to lead to a listing agreement. Those documents were needed to help determine the sales price. This list of materials represents what the buyer is apt to request; documents can vary but generally include the following items.

- Current rent roll
- Lease expirations or aging report
- Operating statements (three prior years and current year to date)
- Current market survey if available
- Copies of all service contracts
- Access to tenant files
- Access to units with advance notification

- List of down units

- List of non-revenue units

- Detailed payroll list showing every employee, their compensation (salary, wage, commissions, free rent) and benefits.

- Current year operating budget.

- An accounting of all deposits on hand (refundable and nonrefundable) including security and any other deposits with separate totals for each.

- Delinquent and prepaid list.

- Three-year occupancy list if available.

- Copies of all marketing materials for prospective tenants.

- Descriptions and breakdown of all fees charged.

- Detailed market rent schedule.

- Standard lease form and all riders and letters that are presented to new tenants.

- Copy of title insurance policy.

- Description of liens against the property.

- As-build survey.

- Complete set of plans and specifications if available.

- Termite report if available.

- Environmental affidavit or prior phase one audit if available.

- Personal property inventory.

- Copies of all recent real and personal property tax bills.

- List of capital expenditures for the past three years.

- Insurance policy incurred bills.

- Copies of the most recent utility bills.

- Certificate of Occupancy if available.

Don't be surprised if the seller or their bookkeeper or accountant can't provide the requested materials or if you receive everything in a shoebox. You have to pay attention to detail, but your seller may be more lax. In addition, your seller may not have the documents, or it's nearly impossible to reproduce them. In this case, try to get everything you can and then copy them and keep a copy in your office. This keeps you from having to collect them again from the seller if one offer falls apart.

IV. Procrastination

Seller procrastination is avoided if the listing agent obtains all the required documents and related information while the property is marketed. Buyer delays, however, can't be so easily overcome.

It may be hard to believe, but sometimes buyers don't behave in accordance with the contract. In fact, most buyers will wait until they know they have a mortgage commitment before they order their environmental inspection, survey and appraisal. The problem is that they now have 5 to 10 days' worth of time to get 30 days' worth of work completed. This situation usually results in the buyers' broker calling and asking for a two-week extension to the closing date. This may unnecessarily sour the deal and make later negotiations more difficult. The key to avoiding this is to make sure everyone is aware of upcoming deadlines.

Either the sellers' or the buyers' broker can distribute a chronology letter to all the concerned parties that contains deadlines as well as contact information. Keeping all the parties to a transaction on the straight and narrow is like rounding up a bag of cats. You will find that brokers routinely tell you that they don't need a chronology letter. Attorneys will assert that you can't tell them what to do or how to do their job, and title companies will say that they have their own internal systems for monitoring details. If you buy that, you will close when they want to close and not when you and your client want to close. You have to be prepared to take over the process and get things done. Things that should have been done by the other sales associate in the transaction.

Refer to the following sample letter before your next deal.

February 1, 2013

Dr. John Buyer
121 Mockingbird Lane
Anywhere, Florida 33308
Re: Purchase of property located at 3000 New Building Lane, Anywhere, FL 33319

Dear Dr. Buyer,

This letter shall serve to delineate the progress of the transaction and set forth the times and dates for performance as indicated by the agreement.

Contract Date:	January 24, 2013
Effective Date:	January 28, 2013
Initial Deposit:	January 31, 2013
Mortgage Application:	February 4, 2013
Due Diligence Documents:	February 6, 2013
Survey:	February 9, 2013
Physical Inspections:	February 28, 2013
Mortgage Commitment:	February 28, 2013
Second Deposit:	March 5, 2013
Closing Date:	March 29, 2013

[Insert here the name, address, phone number and email address for the buyer, seller, both attorneys and the title company.]

Periodically, I will be calling or emailing the buyer's real estate associate to confirm that certain items required in this agreement have been delivered or performed in accordance with the agreement. The performance of some of these items will require written acknowledgement of receipt; we will be watching these items carefully to ensure that the transaction moves forward as smoothly as possible. We will work diligently to eliminate all the traditional issues that need to be resolved prior to a successful closing.

Sincerely,

Tom Agent

V. Rules for Engagement

If you adhere to the following guidelines, you'll exponentially increase your chance of a successful closing. Remember, the contract is only the beginning so pay attention. The devil is in the details.

1. Gather the due diligence materials during the marketing of the property and not after you have an agreement. The buyer will use any delay to push back the closing date, thereby gaining an advantage for themselves.

2. Upon full execution of the agreement, get copies to all parties immediately.

3. Get complete contact information for the buyer, seller, both attorneys, title company, inspection companies, and anyone else involved in the transaction.

4. Provide due diligence materials to the buyer along with a copy of the fully executed contract. Have the buyer sign a printed receipt for the documents so that they can't later say they got them late or never at all.

5. Create a chronology letter with performance due dates and deliver copies to all the interested parties.

6. Schedule events in your calendar so that you can remind the buyer and buyer's agent of due dates and then follow up. Don't be afraid to be a bit of a pain. Remember that the squeaky wheel gets the grease.

7. Keep your broker or manager informed as to the progress, specifically if a party is not performing in accordance with the contract. Do not under any circumstances withhold information thinking you can work it out yourself. If you're wrong, you and your broker could end up looking for an exciting and rewarding new career.

8. Do not practice law unless you're an attorney. If there are legal questions raised, get an attorney involved immediately. Attorneys cost money but the right one will ensure a closing, and that you are paid.

9. Follow up on third-party reports. See if the appraisal is in and if the environmental, roof and electrical inspections have been completed and provided to the parties that are entitled to them.

10. Check with the attorney or title agent regarding the closing schedule. Make sure they have it on their calendar, and that it hasn't gotten lost. Stranger things have happened.

11. Ask for and review the closing statement well before closing. You can't imagine the mistakes that you may find. You don't want to find yourself in a situation in which the commission payment is inaccurate or omitted. Make sure that any required FIRPTA withholding is debited from foreign sellers. If there are tenants, security deposit credits to the buyers need to be reflected.

12. Document everything, even the smallest seemingly insignificant item. You never know when it will come in handy.

13. In the event of an escrow dispute, tell your broker or manager immediately. Don't try to fix it; just report it and follow the lawful instructions of your employer.

14. Never go to the closing. The only thing that will happen is that you will be asked to make a commission reduction. The buyer's attorney will attempt to get his client more money and unless the seller is willing to reduce their "net", guess who the next target is. The only exception is when your broker instructs you to have the company attorney attend with a copy of the original listing, seller's confirmation to pay a commission and the agreement for purchase and sale firmly in his grasp.

Step 10: Starting Over

Once you've completed your first deal, you might be tempted to rest on your laurels for a while. That is not the way to get ahead in this business. Listings are the lifeblood of the commercial broker, and you want to keep the pipeline full. If you carefully read this chapter and follow the recommended practices, you're well on your way to a successful career in commercial real estate.

I. Referrals

A referral is a red carpet rolled directly from a happy client to a new prospect. The credibility is enormous. You have just successfully closed a transaction for a friend, vendor, relative or business associate, and now you are being introduced as a trusted confidant. It doesn't get better than that!

When you are given a referral, you need to do everything humanly possible to ensure that the client's needs are met fully and in a timely fashion. If you fail, you not only lose the referral, but you also lose the original client because you now look like a flake and that reflects poorly on them.

Asking

How do you go about getting referrals? You ask. That seems so simple but with the myriad of other things going through your mind who can remember to ask for the referral? The professional will. The client may even expect it from you. It's almost a point of personal pride: I hired her, and she did a great job for me. I'm sure she'll do the same for you.

Timing

The best time to ask for a referral is after the successful closing of a sale while the seller is still riding high on the post-sale wave, and the buyer is still enjoying his new acquisition. However, you don't want to appear too eager or pushy. Wait and let the dust settle a little; at least until you've cashed the check.

When the time is right, send a hand written, hand addressed, stamped thank you note for his business. You might want to send a post-closing present as well; a bottle of champagne, a fruit basket, or anything that you think might appeal to him is a suitable gift. Allow five days for the card and gift to arrive and then give him a call.

Start the conversation by asking if you can be of any further service. Inquire if he has anything else in mind. This opens the door for the seller to tell you about other properties to sell, and it invites buyers to mention possible new acquisitions.

Be sure to ask if he knows anybody else you might be able to help. If he does, request the contact information and ask him to call the individual and tell him about you, and that you will be calling soon. Then don't forget to follow up. These are golden leads that you don't want to waste.

Written

While you have the seller or buyer on the phone, ask if he would mind writing a letter of recommendation. Do not rely on him to write it. You write it based on his comments; email it to him and ask if he'll sign it and print it out on his own letterhead. If you wait for a client to write it, you might have retired before you receive it.

Once you have the letter, immediately place it in your first appointment binder to show future potential clients. Remember, people believe what they see in writing, and it becomes particularly credible when it comes from a third party. You might even want to create a testimonial page on your website and display them all online. Nothing beats global exposure.

> TIP: If you do a good job, your customers will each tell 10 people. If you do a lousy job, they'll tell 20.

II. Marketing

You want to use whatever means are available to you to create a high business profile. This lets the little guys compete with the big boys on a more even playing field.

Press Releases

Every time you close a sale, send out a press release to all the local papers and trade magazines that cover your market or specialty. If you're not yet familiar with them, try entering the following search criteria in your Internet search engine: <state, county or city> real estate newspaper and <state, county or city> commercial real estate journals. Fill in the name of your state, county or city. These searches are likely to retrieve the names of national journals as well as the regional ones. Take a look at the following press release for a sample that you can modify to suit your own purposes. You can publish a version of this whether you represented the seller or the buyer. Once you get a few published, you may even be interviewed for an article or comments on the market.

> **XYZ Southern Realty Facilitates Warehouse Sale**
>
> *Fort Lauderdale, FL* - John Atlas of XYZ Southern Realty has represented the seller, ABC Commercial Trust, in the sale of a 30,000 square-foot warehouse property located at 1090 New Building Road in Fort Lauderdale. Atlantic DEF Trust purchased the property for $3.4 million.

You never know where people may find you, so don't forget the Internet. Add a Press Release page to your website and paste all the press releases there. You can also publish the information using any of the social media tools that are familiar to you including Facebook and Twitter.

Postcards

Always send out a just sold postcard. If you created a database of properties in your specialty, then you already have the names and addresses of the owners. If you haven't yet done this or if the property was outside of your chosen specialty area, then access the property tax records and search for properties with the same use code as the one you just sold. If your software allows you to export information in a comma or tab delimited format, then do it.

Once you have a suitable address list you can make use of one of the online printing services to design a postcard from scratch or from a system template. Include a photograph of yourself on the card. Upload the address list, schedule a mailing date, supply your credit card information, and the task is done. Express Copy is one online vendor that's reasonably priced and easy to use.

If you do this often enough, the owners in your market begin to recognize your name and face, and you become linked with the product type in their minds.

Phone Calls

Last, but not least, call everyone in the market. If you represented the seller, let the owners of similar properties in your market area know that the property closed and that there are still buyers out there who didn't get a chance to purchase your listing. Refer to the just sold script in chapter three for an example of a sample marketing conversation.

III. Discipline

Real estate sales is a profession that needs constant nurturing. You have to keep the momentum going, or you will find yourself back at square one after every sale. That's not an efficient way of working. Most of us are capable of multitasking so do it. Don't devote 100 percent of your time to working one deal. You need to keep prospecting while you are overseeing the progress of pending transactions. It's not easy to do but there is no other way to succeed in this business.

Discipline is the key. Get out your calendar and schedule your daily tasks. Use an online calendar or a printed page, whichever makes you feel more comfortable. Once you have created your database of properties, you need to schedule time for research, cold calls, proposals and first appointments. If you know what you have to do each day, you can stay organized and productive.

IV. Hierarchy

This book has presented in a clear and concise manner a hierarchy of activities that you need to follow in order to succeed as a commercial real estate salesperson. If you catch yourself staring off into space with nothing to do, remember the following steps: research, cold calling, first appointments, preparing a proposal, presenting the proposal at a second appointment, getting the listing, successfully negotiating an offer, closing the transaction and cashing your commission check. You always need to be involved in one or more of these activities.

Cashing a Check

If you suddenly become aware that you're not in the teller line at the bank waiting to make a deposit, then you had better consult the hierarchy. The process is quite simple; if you're not in a higher level of activity, then you need to regroup and start working again.

Closing a Transaction

If you're not depositing a check, then you need to be at a closing (figuratively speaking) or on your way to one by making sure that the closing statement is correct and that all the reports have been completed. Always be preparing to reach a higher level.

Contracts

In order for you to get to the closing, you need to have contracts. But, getting offers is only half the battle. Those contracts need to be valid, enforceable contracts with a probable buyer, a large deposit and a short due diligence period. If the offers have very long inspection periods and minimal deposits, or the buyer is a neophyte with little or no experience and shaky financials, then turn your attention elsewhere and advise the seller to wait for a more favorable offer.

Listings

Meanwhile, you keep trying to get new listings. Listings are the very lifeblood of the business, and you can't expect to survive in the commercial investment real estate field without inventory. And not just any inventory, but well-priced, deliverable inventory from motivated sellers who are committed to selling the property in the context of today's market. You want to work with sellers who are willing to sell at market value and who don't insist on listing the property at an inflated and unrealistic price.

Presentation

If you find yourself in a position where your inventory is low, there is only one thing to do and that is to be sitting in a second appointment making a listing presentation. You've created a product that sets the stage for the seller to agree to list the property at a reasonable price and terms. If you have a reasonable list price and a motivated seller, move forward and take the listing. The time is right to get started on your next transaction. However, if you feel that the seller's terms don't give you at least a 70 percent chance of closing, reject the listing and move on to the next one.

Proposal

You may be lucky enough to get a listing based on your charm and good looks, but it's not likely. Most property owners want you to crunch the numbers. You'll need to gather the financial information, reconstruct the operating statement, research the comparable sales and rentals, and wrap it all up in a nice package with photographs.

First Appointment

You usually need to communicate with a seller and establish rapport before you have a chance of obtaining a listing from him. The first appointment is where the heavy lifting occurs; this is where you establish the largest portion of your relationship. First impressions matter and you want to arrive 15 minutes early, create rapport (FORM) and conduct a thorough needs analysis (INVEST). You need to be credible, impress the owner with your marketing knowledge and be able to relate it to your prospect's needs and desires. If you succeed, you're given the financials, and you're on your way to creating the proposal. If you fail, you need to find more prospects.

Cold Call

If you find you have nothing in the pipeline, you need to be burning up the phone lines. You need to be getting in front of the decision makers and making your case for a proposal. What is the worst thing that could happen? They hang up. Big deal; get used to it and call the next number in your database.

Research

Follow your daily schedule and when you've completed your allotted time for cold calls, go back to where it all begins. Research is the bedrock of your career, and you need to be filling your database until you have at least 1,000 completely researched records. Part of the process is to get a photograph of every property and personally meet with every owner in your market. If nothing else, you'll meet a lot of people and maybe have a little fun along the way.

This concludes our 10 step program. Take what you've learned and continue to build on it. There's no substitute for experience but understanding the fundamentals should get you off the couch and in front of a computer to begin your research. Best of luck to you all.

Appendix I. Confidentiality Agreement

BUYER CONFIDENTIALITY AGREEMENT

This is a Request for Informational Materials that have been prepared regarding the sale of

_____ ("Property") and are intended solely for

_____ ("Prospective Purchaser") and its limited use in

considering its interest to purchase the Property located in Broward County, Florida from

_____ ("Owner").

XYZ Realty Advisors have prepared a confidential package of information related to the Property. The information is not warranted to be all-inclusive or accurate.

Prospective Purchaser agrees that the information will remain confidential and not disclosed to anyone else or copied without written authorization from XYZ Realty Advisors. The sale of the Property may not be discussed with the staff or tenants without permission from XYZ Realty Advisors. XYZ Realty Advisors represents the Owner and is the only party receiving compensation from the Owner.

The Prospective Purchaser acknowledges that the Owner has no obligation to Prospective Purchaser unless a written purchase agreement is signed and delivered to Owner and Prospective Purchaser.

The Owner may terminate discussions with any party without notice. Prospective Purchaser agrees to immediately return the information package to XYZ Realty Advisors if the transaction fails to close.

ACKNOWLEDGED AND AGREED ON: _____
                                                            DATE

_____   _____
Prospective Purchaser/Entity (Print Name)   Authorized Signature for Purchaser/Entity

_____   _____
Street Address   Purchaser Entity (Print Name)

_____   _____   _____
City, State and Zip Code   Phone Number   Email

RETURN TO: XYZ Realty Advisors   Email: jdoe@xyzrealtyadvisors.com

DATE RECEIVED: _____

APPROVED BY: _____

DATE APPROVED: _____

Appendix II. Cooperating Broker's Agreement

COOPERATING BROKER CONFIDENTIALITY AND REGISTRATION AGREEMENT

THIS CONFIDENTIALITY AGREEMENT ("Agreement") is made and agreed to by

_____ ("Cooperating Broker") and XYZ Realty Advisors ("Exclusive Listing Broker") regarding the property known as

_____ (Property"). This obligation of confidentiality undertaken pursuant to this Agreement shall survive any future agreement with the Owner.

XYZ Realty Advisors have prepared a confidential package of information related to the Property for the Cooperating Broker. The information is not warranted to be all-inclusive or accurate.

Cooperating Broker agrees that the information will remain confidential and not disclosed to anyone else or copied without written authorization from XYZ Realty Advisors. The sale of the Property may not be discussed with the staff or tenants without permission from XYZ Realty Advisors. XYZ Realty Advisors is the sole representative of the Owner.

If the sale of the Property closes and the Owner pays XYZ Realty Advisors the commission, XYZ Realty Advisors agrees to pay a Cooperating Broker Fee in the amount of _____ (%) of the total selling price to Cooperating Broker.

The Cooperating Broker must register all Buyers prior to receiving the information package. If the Cooperating Broker doesn't register the Buyer, they won't receive the Cooperating Broker Fee.

Cooperating Broker: _____

Agent: _____

Address: _____

Telephone: _____

Email: _____

By: _____

Date: _____

Appendix III. Exclusive Representation Agreement

EXCLUSIVE COMMERCIAL BUYER/BROKER AGREEMENT

THIS EXCLUSIVE BUYER/BROKER AGREEMENT (Agreement") is signed on

_____ ("Effective Date"), by _____

whose address is _____

_____ (Broker)

and _____ ,whose address is

_____

_____(Client)

Client chooses Broker as exclusive agent to assist Client in securing real property. The Client will refer all inquiries related to the property to the Broker.

This agreement begins on the Effective Date and terminates at 11:59 p.m. on the last day of _____, 20____ This Agreement may be canceled prior to this date only by the written agreement..

Client desires to purchase property for a $_____ price range and the following terms and location.

_____

_____

115

_____

_____

The Broker agrees to identify properties, handle negotiations and follow through on details. In return, the Client agrees to pay Broker a commission if the Client purchases, options or signs a letter of intent to purchase a property even if the transaction closes after the contract terminates. A commission is also due within _____ months after this contract terminates if the Client purchases a property that the Broker identified for the Client during the time the Agreement was in effect. The Broker does not have to be the procuring cause to be owed the commission.

If the Broker receives a Seller-paid commission, that amount will be deducted from the Client's commission obligation. The Client agrees to pay the Broker a fixed fee for each property of $_____ or _____ percent of the purchase price. The Client also agrees to immediately pay the Broker a nonrefundable $_____ retainer fee, which will be deducted from the Client's commission obligation if a sales transaction closes.

Client agrees to pay for products or services that are ordered by the Broker on the Client's behalf. Any controversies relating to this Agreement will be settled by binding arbitration and Client or Broker can terminate this agreement by providing twenty-one days written notice.

Client: _____   Broker: _____

Appendix IV.   Using the HP 10BII Financial Calculator

The following links are a useful resource for understanding the full functionality of the calculator. You can also download an app.

Website: http://www.educalc.net/1268086.page	Calculator photo
Website: http://h10032.www1.hp.com/ctg/Manual/bpia5213.pdf	Calculator user manual

I.   Basic Concepts

If you don't have a calculator with you, but you do have a computer, use the links to follow along with the examples in this chapter. The answers to the problems are at the end of this appendix.

Keys

- Shift Key (GOLD Key)

    The GOLD key is third from the bottom along the left side. Click this to access the functions in gold on the keyboard. The word Shift appears in the lower right hand corner of the display screen when pressed. Press it again to turn it off.

- On/Off

    ON key is bottom left corner. To turn the calculator off, press GOLD then OFF (on the ON key)

- Arithmetic

    The basic math symbols are on the lower right side

- Registers

The calculator operates on a series of financial registers: N, I/YR, PV, PMT and FV.

N is the number of periods.

For example, for a 30 year loan with 12 payments per year, N is 360. To set the number of monthly payments enter: 12 GOLD P/YR (the PMT key). You can check this value by pressing GOLD C ALL (The C key. The C ALL clears all the registers except for P/YR). The display will show 12 if you set it correctly. Now enter 30 GOLD xP/YR (the N key) and the screen should display 360.

To check any register press RCL (for Recall) and then the register. For example, if you entered the data for a 30 year loan with 12 payments per year, RCL GOLD P/YR should display 12 (payments per year), RCL GOLD xP/YR displays 30 (loan term) and RCL N displays 360 (payment periods).

I/YR is the interest rate.

Enter 5 I/YR to set the interest rate to 5 percent.

PV is the Present Value.

If you receive a $120,000 loan, the PV is $120,000. If you are investing a lump sum of 1,050, PV is -1,050. Money you receive is positive, and payments you make are negative. To enter a payment: 1,050 +/- PV. The +/- key makes the number negative and the screen displays -1,050. PV is used when there is only one lump sum amount of money.

PMT is the loan payment.

A loan payment is calculated in the first exercise. PMT is used when there is more than one payment.

FV is the Future Value

If you have a fully amortized loan, the FV is $0. We will use this register in the following problems.

Appendix IV Using the Financial Calculator

- Display Function

    To set the number of decimal places to 3 press GOLD DISP (the = key) 3. Your screen should display 3.000. Set the display to whatever precision you prefer. It doesn't affect how the number is stored internally.

Calculations

These are the types of calculations that you will use in the practice of commercial real estate. Except for mortgage calculations, this is very different from residential real estate so practice until you are comfortable. Chapter 5 and this appendix have useful examples.

- Mortgage Payment

- Cash Flows

- Compounding

- Discounting

- Net Present Value (NPV)

- Present Value (PV)

- Internal Rate of Return (IRR)

TIP: Set the value for each of the five registers to 0 before performing any new calculation.

Try working out the following problems. If you get stuck, the answers are at the end of this appendix.

II. Exercise One

Problem

A borrower wants to borrow $125,000 to buy a house. The lender says they will make the loan based on a 30 year amortization with a 10% interest rate per year.

What is the borrower's payment going to be? Do we have enough information to calculate the answer?

Use Registers to Diagram

GOLD P/YR _____

N _____

I/YR _____

PV _____

PMT _____

FV _____

III. Exercise Two

Problem

Amortize a mortgage for a single payment, the principal portion, the interest portion, or even a balloon payment.

First, let's use our prior example. The borrower takes out a new loan of $125,000 amortized for 30 years and bearing interest at 10% per annum.

Our payment was $1,096.96 per month. Right?

1. What is the interest portion of the 60th monthly payment?

2. What would be the principal portion of the payment?

3. What would be the balloon payment due?

Remember the two methods for calculating a balloon payment; there is the "long-hand" version and the "short-hand" version. The difference in the rounding is negligible to the extent that it is not even worth mentioning.

IV. Exercise Three

Problem

If we are offered an annuity that will pay $200,000 each year for the next 10 years, what would we be willing to pay for it today...in cash? This calculation is called discounting.

1	$200,000
2	$200,000
3	$200,000
4	$200,000
5	$200,000
6	$200,000
7	$200,000
8	$200,000
9	$200,000
10	$200,000

GOLD P/YR _____

N _____

I/YR _____

PV _____

PMT _____

FV _____

* You can only use the PMT register for EVEN cash flows. For uneven cash flows, you need to use the Cash Flow Journal or CFJ key.

V. Exercise Four

If you won the lottery would you be better off taking the cash and paying the taxes or taking the annuity?

Problem

The class purchases a winning lottery ticket, and the jackpot is $40 million paid over 20 years. So, effectively, we would get $2 million each year for the next 20 years. Sounds like an annuity doesn't it?

Would we be better taking it all in cash now or over the 20 years? Well, it depends. It depends on what "discount rate" the lottery commission is going to use. Let's suppose they use an 8% discount rate.

1. What would we end up getting before income taxes?

2. If we did get the lump sum, suppose we invested it at the same rate. What would happen?

3. Is there a difference? If so, why?

Diagram

N _____

I/YR _____

PV _____

PMT _____

FV _____

VI. Exercise Five

You've probably heard of compound interest, but maybe never quite understood it. This example should make things clearer for you.

Problem

You've had a banner year and you're looking at putting some money away for retirement. You want to know what it would grow to if you simply tucked it away and forgot about it for 30 years.

1. What happens if we use a 6% compounding rate?

2. What happens if we use 8%, 10% or even 12%?

3. If there was a change, explain why.

4. Will you have a nice little nest egg?

Diagram

N   _____

I/YR   _____

PV   _____

PMT   _____

FV   _____

VII. Exercise Six

Problem

So much for our banner year! Tuition, mortgages, the stock market and your new car have all absorbed more cash than expected. So, instead of a lump sum, what if we make an annual deposit in our retirement account. How about $20,000 annually for the next 30 years?

1. What do we have to retire on at a 6% rate of interest?

2. What would we have at 8%, 10% or 12%?

Diagram

N   _____

I/YR   _____

PV   _____

PMT   _____

FV   _____

VIII. Exercise Seven

Problem

How about a real world example? A client has asked you to look at an investment property and analyze the "Annual Property Operating Data" for the subject property. One thing you noticed is that the agent marketing the property didn't put in any "reserves for replacement" and it's evident that the roof is going to need to be replaced in 5 years. What should we do?

The building has roughly 10,000 square feet of roofing and a competent roofing contractor has told us that a roof costs $3.00 per square foot, but that is in today's dollars. What will it cost 5 years hence, and if we don't want to get caught, what should we start reserving today?

Part one is easy....it's just compounding

N　　　_____

I/YR　_____

PV　　_____

PMT　_____

FV　　_____

Now, what do we have to put away each year for the next 5 years to arrive at that amount at a 6% compounding rate?

N　　　_____

I/YR　_____

PV　　_____

PMT　_____

FV　　_____

IX. Exercise Eight

Problem

Did you ever wonder why a car dealer was so anxious to lease you a car rather than have you buy a car? It's because they make more money! When they lease a car they "sell" you the vehicle for $X and they tell you if you bring it back in better condition than when you leased it, you will have a residual of $X. We'll leave the "Cap-Cost Reduction" out of the equation for simplicity's sake; however, for informational purposes that cap-cost reduction is like points to a lender...pre-paid profit!

The sales price is $35,000 as equipped. Your monthly payment is $539 for a three year lease. When you return the leased vehicle in pristine condition, the residual is $25,000. Can we calculate the interest rate you are paying?

Diagram

GOLD P/YR _____

N _____

I/YR _____

PV _____

PMT _____

FV _____

Is leasing this car a good deal?

X. Exercise Nine

Here is an example of how you can save thousands, tens or even hundreds of thousands of dollars in interest payments on all your mortgages. Let's refer to the earliest example way back when we started this adventure. Remember, we have a $125,000 mortgage for 30 years at 10% interest per year. Here's what it would look like broken out.

Period	Payment	Interest	Principal	Balance
1	$1096.96	$1,041.67	$55.29	$124,944.71
2	$1096.96	$1,041.21	$55.75	$124,888.96
3	$1096.96	$1,040.74	$56.22	$124,832.74
4	$1096.96	$1,040.27	$56.69	$124,776.05
5	$1096.96	$1,039.80	$57.16	$124,718.89
6	$1096.96	$1,039.32	$57.64	$124,661.25
7	$1096.96	$1,038.84	$58.12	$124,603.13
8	$1096.96	$1,038.36	$58.60	$124,544.53
9	$1096.96	$1,037.87	$59.09	$124,485.44
10	$1096.96	$1,037.38	$59.58	$124,425.86
Total	$10,969.64	$10,395.46	$574.14	

Now, pay attention because this is worth the price of admission! If you can write a check to your lender for $574.14 (the principal reduction after the first 10 months) and write "principal only" in the memo, you will save yourself the $10,395.46 interest charge.

Here are two cautionary pieces of advice: 1) check to make sure that you are permitted to prepay your mortgage. Some flaky new mortgages prohibit prepayment after 20% of the outstanding principal has been remitted in one year, and 2) this does NOT relieve you of any responsibility for the next several months payments. It does, however, shorten the maturity of the loan and save you huge, enormous sums of money.

XI. Problem Solutions

Exercise One

A borrower wants to borrow $125,000 to buy a house. The lender says they will make the loan based on a 30 year amortization with a 10% interest rate per year.

What is the borrower's payment going to be? Do we have enough information to calculate the answer?

Use Registers to Diagram

GOLD P/YR	12
GOLD xP/YR	30
N	displays 360 (or you could enter 360 N and nothing for GOLD xP/YR)
I/YR	10
PV	$125,000
PMT	? solve for PMT
FV	0

Solution: Press PMT and -1,096.96 should display. If you didn't get this, use the RCL key to view the content of the five registers. Remember to enter the number first and then press the register key. The answer is negative because it is money you are paying.

Problem: Without clearing any of the registers, what is the monthly loan payment if the interest rate is 12%?

Solution: Enter 12 I/YR PMT and the display should read -1,285.77

Problem: What is the loan amount (PV) if the monthly payment is -1,096.96 (PMT), 10% interest for a 30 year loan? Remember that PMT must be a negative number (use the +/- key to change sign)

Solution: Press PV and 124,999.49 should display. Get it? If not, check the value of the registers.

Exercise Two

Amortize a mortgage for a single payment, the principal portion, the interest portion, or even a balloon payment. First, let's use our prior example. The borrower takes out a new loan of $125,000 amortized for 30 years and bearing interest at 10% per annum. Our payment was $1,096.96 per month. Right?

1. What is the interest portion of the 60th monthly payment?

2. What would be the principal portion of the payment?

3. What would be the balloon payment due after 5 years?

If we need to find the value of the interest payment or principal reduction for a particular month, we need to use the GOLD AMORT key (on the FV key.) If we are trying to find the value of a future payment, we are solving for FV and can do this through the AMORT or FV register. Ready?

Verify (RCL) that the registers contain N=360, I/YR =10, PV = 125,000, FV =0, P/YR=12

Solution 1: We want to check the P&I (principal and interest) components of the monthly $1,096.96 mortgage payment for the end of the 5th year (month 60)

RCL PMT	this should be -1,096.96.
60 INPUT 60 GOLD AMORT	the INPUT ley is on the top left side
Press =	-90.22 principal reduction in month 60
Press =	-1006.74 interest payment in month 60
Press =	120,718,245 loan balance in month 60
1 INPUT 60 GOLD AMORT = = =	displays total P&I paid and loan balance after 5 years

Solution 2 Shortcut: Find the balloon payment at the end of five years (month 60)

60 N

FV   -120,718,245.

Exercise Three

If we are offered an annuity that will pay $200,000 each year for the next 10 years, what would we be willing to pay for it today...in cash? This calculation is called discounting.

1	$200,000
2	$200,000
3	$200,000
4	$200,000
5	$200,000
6	$200,000
7	$200,000
8	$200,000
9	$200,000
10	$200,000

Solution: Annuities are usually paid annually, so we need to change that first

GOLD P/YR   1

N   10

I/YR   8 % is the chosen discount rate

PV   ? solve for this

PMT   200,000 this is positive because we are receiving this money

FV   0

PV is -1,342,016.28. We would pay this amount now for a $2,000,000 income stream that's paid out as $200,000 annual payments over 10 years. The 8% discount rate is the return on the investment that we want in order to compensate us for inflation, opportunity cost and taxes.

Exercise Four

The class purchases a winning lottery ticket, and the jackpot is $40 million paid over 20 years. So, effectively, we would get $2 million each year for the next 20 years. Sounds like an annuity doesn't it? Would we be better taking it all in cash now or over the 20 years? Well, it depends. It depends on what "discount rate" the lottery commission is going to use. Let's suppose they use an 8% discount rate.

1. What would we end up getting before income taxes?

2. If we did get the lump sum money, suppose we invested it at the same rate. What would happen?

3. Is there a difference? If so, why?

Diagram

GOLD P/YR	1
N	20
I/YR	8 % is the chosen discount rate
PV	? solve for this
PMT	2,000,000
FV	0

Solution 1: PV is -19,636,294.82 It is negative because it's from the point of view of the lottery commission. $19,636,294.82 lump sum payment instead of $40 million paid over 20 years.

Solution 2: Now invest $19,636,294.82 at 8% for 20 years without clearing the registers.

PMT	0 use PV when only one deposit; PMT is for multiple payments
FV	91,523,928.57 which is much better than $40 million

Problem: What if we didn't take the lump sum and instead invested the $2,000,000 each year for 20 years at 8% return? Solve for FV.

PV	0
PMT	- 2,000,000 this is a PMT because 2,000,000 is deposited annually
FV	? FV = 91,523,928.60

Exercise Five

You've had a banner year and you're looking at putting some money away for retirement. You want to know what it would grow to if you simply tucked it away and forgot about it for 30 years.

1. What happens if we use a 6% compounding rate?

2. What happens if we use 8%, 10% or even 12%?

3. If there was a change, explain why.

4. Will you have a nice little nest egg?

Solution 1; Solve for FV

GOLD P/YR	1
N	30
I/YR	6
PV	-20,000 we are going to make one $20,000 investment
PMT	0
FV	? $114,869.82

Solution 2:

I/YR	8
FV	? $201,253.14

Solution 3:

I/YR	10
FV	? $348,988.05

Solution 4:

I/YR	12
FV	? $599,198.44

Exercise 6

So much for our banner year! Tuition, mortgages, the stock market and your new car have all absorbed more cash than expected. So, instead of a lump sum, what if we make an annual deposit in our retirement account. How about $20,000 annually for the next 30 years?

1. What do we have to retire on at a 6% rate of interest?

2. What would we have at 8%, 10% or 12%?

Solution 1:

GOLD P/YR	1
N	30
I/YR	6
PV	0
PMT	-20,000
FV	? $1,581,63.72

Solution 2:

I/YR	8
FV	? $2,265,664.22

Solution 3:

I/YR	10
FV	? $3,289,880.46

Solution 4:

I/YR	12
FV	? $4,826,653.69

Exercise 7

The building has roughly 10,000 square feet of roofing and a competent roofing contractor has told us that a roof costs $3.00 per square foot, but that is in today's dollars. What will it cost 5 years hence, and if we don't want to get caught, what should we start reserving today?

Solution 1: Solve for FV

GOLD P/YR	1
N	5
I/YR	6 assume 6% interest
PV	-30,000
PMT	0
FV	? $40,146.77

Now, what do we have to put away each year for the next 5 years to arrive at that amount at a 6% compounding rate?

Solution 2: Solve for PMT

N	5
I/YR	6
PV	0
PMT	? -$7,121.89 each year for 5 years
FV	40,146.77

Exercise Eight

The sales price is $35,000 as equipped. Your monthly payment is $539 for a three year lease. When you return the leased vehicle in pristine condition, the residual is $25,000. Can we calculate the interest rate you are paying?

Solution:

GOLD P/YR	12
N	36
I/YR	? - 33.45 %
PV	- 35,000
PMT	-539
FV	25,000

You actually borrowed $10,000 for 3 years ($35,000 sale price - $25,000 residual) and paid a whopping 33.45 % interest on the money. Wow!

CPSIA information can be obtained
at www.ICGtesting.com
Printed in the USA
LVHW041058301118
598766LV00021B/432